Other works by Robert St. John

Deep South Parties

Deep South Staples

# New South Grilling

# New South Grilling

Fresh and Exciting Recipes from the Third Coast

## Robert St. John

HYPERION

NEW YORK

ISBN: 978-1-4013-0837-7

Hyperion books are available for special promotions, premiums, or corporate training. For details contact Michael Rentas, Proprietary Markets, Hyperion, 77 West 66th Street, 12th floor, New York, New York 10023, or call 212–456–0133.

FIRST EDITION

10  9  8  7  6  5  4  3  2  1

Design and composition by Ralph Fowler / rlf design

To Jill, Holleman, and Harrison

# Contents

# Acknowledgments

A million thanks to Linda Nance, chef de cuisine, Purple Parrot Café—for recipe testing, hand holding, and wise culinary counsel.

Joey DeLeo—photographer, art director, and newly adopted Southerner, for his beautiful photographs, and a fun-filled two weeks without a food stylist, without an air conditioner, and without a net.

Rebecca Whittington and Justin Jordan—for long, long, long hours during the photo shoot while having to work with a first-time food stylist (me).

Linda Nance's Culinary Militia—Chefs Jeremy Noffke, Scott Strickland, Rebecca Whittington, Justin Ferguson, Colby Stark, and Charlene Rogers, for early, early mornings firing up the coals in the busiest little makeshift test kitchen in the South.

Leslie Wells—the best damn editor, period, and officially the most patient woman on the planet.

Will Schwalbe—for his constant faith, guidance, support, and vision (and also for sending DeLeo my way).

Mitchell Waters—my literary agent, without whom these books would still be dreams swimming around in the dark depths of my twisted little brain.

Stacey Andrews and Maria Keyes—who handle the day-to-day craziness that is my life and work.

Clint Taylor, New South Restaurant Group, Managing Partner—for continuing to hold down the fort.

Fred Carl, Carol Puckett, Dale Persons, and Jane Crump of Mississippi's own Viking Range Corporation, for their continued support, and for manufacturing the finest outdoor grilling equipment, bar none.

Jill, Holleman, and Harrison—for giving me the two best job titles I'll ever have: husband and father.

# New South Grilling

# Introduction

This is the cookbook that almost burned my restaurant to the ground.

When I write a cookbook, the recipe testing is typically done in my restaurant kitchens at the Purple Parrot Café and Crescent City Grill in my hometown of Hattiesburg, Mississippi. To make sure the process doesn't get in the way of normal restaurant operations (if there is such an animal), we begin recipe testing very early in the morning.

During the initial cookbook-testing months, Purple Parrot Café chef de cuisine and chief recipe tester Linda Nance usually arrives around 3 A.M., and begins to get the day's *mise en place* together for the testing chefs. Throughout the crunch period she is the only person—save the cleaning crew—in the building. She uses this "alone time" to get her portion of the work done without outside interference.

I am usually at my desk, writing recipes, rewording descriptions and procedures, and performing the dozens of other tasks involved in putting together a cookbook. Around 5 A.M. I usually check in with Linda to discuss the day's recipe-testing schedule, cover any ingredient changes or modifications, and to see how the day's recipe prep is going. Around 7 A.M., breakfast is served—whatever recipe we are working on that day—and occasionally the dish is perfect the first time out. Most times we go back to the drawing board a few times before the recipe is perfected enough to be published.

A grilling book was a new challenge for us. We grill hundreds of pounds of fish, chicken, steaks, and burgers every day, but we aren't set up to do scaled-down, home-style grilling in our restaurant kitchens. Most of the recipes in this book were prepared on grills and smokers on the loading dock behind the restaurant or in my backyard at home.

At the restaurant, when we light charcoal for the grill or smoker, we place the charcoal in a sauté pan and then place it under the salamander (a large gas-fired broiler used to finish dishes and melt cheese). After four or five minutes, the coals are hot enough to transfer to the smoker or grill. It saves a few minutes, and a few minutes are important at 4 A.M.

Back to the aforementioned restaurant fire . . . Early one morning, midway through the recipe-testing phase of this book, the ever-reliable Chef Linda placed a pan of charcoal under the salamander as we have done a thousand times before. For some reason on this particular morning, she was distracted (she might say extremely focused) and she forgot about the charcoal. Alone in the restaurant and oblivious to what was occurring behind the line, she went to work in the kitchen office. When she stepped back into the kitchen, the pan of coals in the salamander was on fire. Before she could run behind the line, the entire salamander was on fire and the flames were getting higher and hotter with each passing second.

The salamander is mounted high on the wall behind the char-broiler. At first Linda tried to put the fire out with kitchen towels. At this point, the situation looked as if she might be able to keep the elaborate hood-mounted fire extinguisher system from tripping, which would shut the restaurant down for at least twenty-four hours. But the towels did nothing more than fan the flames.

When she realized that towels weren't getting the job done, Linda grabbed one of the heavy rubber mats in the service area, jumped up on the stove, and tried to smother the four-foot flames. Consequently, the mat caught on fire, and melted rubber began dripping on her arms. At the last moment, a member of the cleaning crew—and the only other person in the building—ran up with a handheld fire extinguisher and doused the blaze.

"The good news is I'm OK, and the restaurant didn't burn to the ground. The bad news is—we're going to need a new salamander" were the words that greeted me when I arrived in the kitchen that morning. Had Linda not walked out of the office when she did, I would be writing this introduction from my home study and not my restaurant office.

*"The no-stick grilling marinades will change forever the way you season food for grilling and the way you grill it."*

A fire is a restaurateur's worst nightmare. Luckily, our restaurants survived the salamander-charcoal fiasco to serve customers another day. Something happened after that incident. A new focus spread throughout the testing crew. The fire that almost was manifested into a fire in my belly, and my desire to create a new and unique grilling cookbook grew even stronger. It was also around this time that we began using a metal chimney starter to light the outdoor grills.

Recipe testing for my previous book, *Deep South Parties*, was set to begin the day Hurricane Katrina swept through my hometown with 130-mph winds, blowing the second floor off of the restaurant and shutting us down for several weeks. So, in the larger scheme of life and work, a fire that almost was is no sweat.

This book might have had a troubled beginning, but I believe that the final product is singular, unique, and the most solid and tasteful collection of recipes I have published to date.

Hopefully, this is not your average, ordinary, run-of-the-mill, list-dozens-of-barbeque-sauce-recipes-and-fifty-ways-to-grill-a-steak cookbook. You won't find a lot of elaborately illustrated and detailed grilling instructions within these pages. There are plenty of volumes on bookstore shelves that cover the intricacies of grilling all manner of beef, chicken, and pork—this isn't one of them.

If you have purchased this book, the odds are high that you are already a well-versed grilling enthusiast and have several cookbooks in your collection that do a much better job of covering grilling basics than I ever could. This volume assumes that you already know how to light charcoal, rotate food, keep it away from direct flames, and make crosshatch marks. We won't cover those topics. We will, however, offer new ways to season, marinate, and prepare grilled food.

Some of the most useful recipes you'll find in this book are the no-stick grilling marinades. As a kid growing up in South Mississippi, spending summers in fish camps near the Gulf of Mexico, I saw all manner of culinary oddities. Some were long-standing traditions passed down several generations; others were developed out of spur-of-the-moment necessity when suitable ingredients weren't in the fish camp pantry.

The first time I saw mustard spread on a redfish filet before it was dredged in cornmeal for frying, I thought that my grandfather had done it because there was no egg wash available. That might have been the case at one point in his life, but somewhere along the way, someone figured out that it was a great way to fry fish. The mustard served as a great adhesive for the cornmeal and it lost its tangy bite in the frying process. He always fried fish using that method.

The no-stick grilling marinades work under the same principle. They were originally developed out of either necessity or boredom. The marinades aren't pretty, and the flavor is too strong for them to be eaten as a stand-alone condiment. Nevertheless, the no-stick grilling marinades will change forever the way you season food for grilling and the way you grill it.

*"I suddenly realized that—when cooking at home—I wasn't a chef in a restaurant, but a dad who cooks on the grill. It's the best job I'll ever have . . ."*

Many people are scared to grill fish over live charcoal. They might have tried once or twice, but the fish stuck to the grill grates and burned too easily. Consequently, they gave it up and dusted off the frying pan. Brush the no-stick grilling marinade on a fish filet, place the filet on well-cleaned grill grates, cook it for a few minutes, and it will flip perfectly every time.

The spice blends and dry rubs in this book are easy and flavorful. They will help turn your typical salt-and-pepper-seasoned food into bold-flavored dishes that you, your family, your friends, and guests will love. Anyone can grill a steak, but as long as you purchase the best beef available, what will separate your steak from all of the others is method and seasoning. This book is short on method, but long on seasoning.

Grilling outdoors is one of the most socially interactive culinary activities I do. At a party, everyone hangs out in my kitchen. At an outdoor barbeque, everyone hangs out at my grill. It's always more fun outside—there's more room, the scenery changes, and the ceiling is much higher.

The recipes listed herein draw their inspiration from several places. Some have been developed in my restaurant kitchens over the last twenty years, and have been subsequently scaled down for home use. Some are backyard grilling staples that I have been preparing since my teenage years, and others were created especially for this collection.

There are a lot of grilled seafood recipes in this book. I live one hour due north of the Gulf of Mexico. I grew up spending my summers on the Gulf Coast. Grilling and seafood have been synonymous dining partners my entire life. Don't be afraid to grill seafood. Use the no-stick grilling marinades and you'll be adding more flavor and keeping your cardiologist happy at the same time.

There are a few tools you will need to prepare the recipes in this book. Odds are you already have most of them. If you don't, you've got something lying around the house that will suffice. A grill screen is a must when grilling items such as shrimp or small vegetables. If you don't have a screen or grate that was specifically designed to be used on an outdoor grill, go to the garage and find a suitable substitute.

We have already established the fact that you are not a beginning griller. Here are a few tips that you probably already know, but we'll cover them, anyway.

## The New South Grill Basics

1. Keep grill grates cleaned and oiled. (Clean grates with a wire grill brush after every use; use an oil-soaked dish towel to grease the grates before turning on/firing up the grill.)

2. Never use lighter fluid or charcoal already soaked in lighter fluid. For the best-tasting grill food, use only pure hardwood lump charcoal.

3. Know in advance the grill temperature required for the dish you're preparing.

4. Whether cooking with gas or charcoal—always preheat the grill.

5. Know where the hot spots and the cool spots are, and use them to your advantage.

6. Heat means hot coals, not high flames.

7. Leave food alone while it's grilling—turn over once.

8. Don't underestimate the value of the grill's lid. A closed lid adds flavor, regulates heat, and prevents flare-ups.

9. Don't pierce meat with a fork or knife to check if it's done. Learn how to grill by touch.

10. Barbeque sauce always goes on at the last minute, if at all.

The photography in this book is gorgeous. Full credit for the beautifully photographed recipes goes to Joey DeLeo, who spent two weeks on my front porch and in my backyard enduring the grueling Mississippi heat with his 17-megapixel Canon and an Apple laptop. In retrospect, his biggest challenge was not how to shoot the food, what plates to use, or how to garnish the center-of-the-plate items, but teaching his first-time food stylist—me—how it is supposed to be done.

Preparing food for friends or restaurant customers comes easy to me. Preparing food to be photographed was an entirely new experience. Three days into the two-week shoot, I was wondering how someone could remain

> *"Never use lighter fluid or charcoal already soaked in lighter fluid. For the best-tasting grill food, use only pure hardwood lump charcoal."*

sane and make a living doing the slow, stressful, and meticulous work of a food stylist. By the end of the first week, I was looking forward to the next day and to hopefully fulfilling the role of food stylist for my next book.

All of the recipes in this book were tested on a Viking 53-inch Ultra-Premium Grill with Side Burners and Tru Sear, a Viking VCQS C4 Outdoor Cooker and Smoker, a Viking VEOS Outdoor Smoker Oven, and a Weber One-Touch Silver Grill. Like having a great sous-chef at your side, using the best grilling equipment you can afford will help you more than any of the after-market gadgets and trinkets found in foodie shops.

As with all non-baking-type cooking, most of these grilling recipes should be viewed as suggestions or starting points before adding your favorite ingredients and techniques. Substitute freely. Find out what works for you and add it to the process. None of these recipes are written in stone. Creativity is what makes cooking fun; sharing the finished result with others is what makes life more enjoyable.

I first started thinking about writing a grilling cookbook around the same time that my fatherhood status kicked into fifth gear. It was in the early days after the birth of my second child. I suddenly realized that—when cooking at home—I wasn't a chef in a restaurant, but a dad who cooks on the grill. It's the best job I'll ever have, and there's no chance of burning down my kitchen when I'm outside.

# Party Food

# Grilled Fish Tacos with Three Sauces

This is one of my favorite recipes in the book . . . no accident why it's listed first. Fresh tortillas work best. Don't use oily, strong-flavored fish. Be careful when grilling tortillas; keep them away from direct flames as they burn easily. Use more cilantro for a more flavorful taco.

2 tsp cumin

1 tsp coriander

1 tsp chili powder

1 tsp granulated garlic

2 tsp kosher salt

⅛ tsp cayenne pepper

2 lbs mahimahi, cut into four 8-ounce steaks

TO SERVE

24 corn tortillas

2 cups thinly shredded green cabbage

2 cups thinly shredded red cabbage

Combine seasonings, sprinkle fish with seasoning, cover, and refrigerate for 1 hour.

Prepare the grill. Grill over direct high heat until the fish is done but not dry, 5–7 minutes.

Allow the fish to cool slightly, then cut into finger-sized 1–2-oz strips.

TO SERVE: Spread 1 tablespoon of Avocado Mayonnaise (recipe follows) in the center of a corn tortilla. Lay 2–3 pieces of fish on top of the mayo, top with shredded cabbage, and then with either the Pineapple Pico de Gallo or the Sweet Corn and Black Bean Salsa (recipes follow).

YIELD: Tacos for 6–8 people

(continued)

# Avocado Mayonnaise

3 egg yolks

2 tsp kosher salt

1 tsp Dijon mustard

½ tsp cumin

½ tsp coriander

2 avocados, ripe

2 Tbl lime juice

2 Tbl white vinegar

¾ cup canola oil

¼ cup sliced green onions,
    paper thin

1 Tbl chopped cilantro

It is very important to use ripe avocados for this recipe.

Place the egg yolks, salt, mustard, cumin, and coriander in a food processor.

Peel and dice the avocados. Turn on the food processor and begin adding the ripe avocado pieces. Add the lime juice and vinegar. Once the avocado is completely pureed, slowly pour the oil into the processor. If the mixture becomes too thick, use a small amount of warm water to thin it down. Once all the oil has been incorporated, transfer the mayonnaise to a mixing bowl. Stir in the green onions and cilantro. Refrigerate until needed.

YIELD: 2½ cups

# Pineapple Pico de Gallo

1½ cups small dice fresh
    tomatoes

¼ cup small dice red onions

2 Tbl thinly sliced green onions

½ tsp minced fresh garlic

2 Tbl chopped cilantro

2 tsp minced fresh jalapeños,
    seeds removed

1 cup small dice pineapple

1 tsp lime juice

½ tsp salt

Combine all ingredients and refrigerate until ready to serve. Best if made 2–3 hours in advance.

YIELD: 3 cups

# Sweet Corn and Black Bean Salsa

1 Tbl olive oil

¼ cup minced yellow onion

2 tsp minced garlic

½ tsp salt

½ tsp cumin

¼ tsp coriander

⅛ tsp dry oregano

1 can Rotel tomatoes
    (10 ounces)

1 cup drained and rinsed
    canned black beans

1 cup fresh sweet corn cut
    from the cob

¼ cup thinly sliced green
    onions

2 tsp fresh lime juice

Place the olive oil in a small stainless steel sauce pot over medium heat. Add the onion, garlic, salt, cumin, coriander, and oregano to the warm oil and cook for 5 minutes, stirring often to prevent burning. Add in the Rotel tomatoes and allow the mixture to simmer 2–3 minutes. Add in the black beans and corn, and cook 5 more minutes. Stir in the thinly sliced green onions and lime juice, and remove from the heat.

YIELD: 3 cups

*"Be careful when grilling tortillas;
keep them away from direct flames
as they burn easily."*

# Grilled Shrimp Tacos

For best results and ease of preparation, use a grill screen when cooking the shrimp. If you don't have a grill screen, skewer the shrimp so they won't fall through the grill. If you're short on time, substitute all sour cream for the crème fraîche.

⅓ cup No-stick Grilling Marinade for Shrimp (page 209)

⅓ cup pineapple juice

54 large shrimp (21–25 count), peeled and deveined

2 tsp kosher salt

1 tsp freshly ground black pepper

1 tsp ground cumin

½ tsp coriander

1 tsp chili powder

18 corn tortillas

1½ cups shredded green leaf lettuce

1½ cups shredded red cabbage

1½ cups shredded green cabbage

Fresh Fruit Pico de Gallo, to taste

Jalapeño and Roasted Garlic Crème Fraîche, to taste

Prepare grill for direct high heat cooking.

In a large mixing bowl, mix the shrimp marinade and pineapple juice. Place shrimp in the bowl and toss with the marinade, coating well. Marinate for 30 minutes.

Combine the salt, pepper, cumin, coriander, and chili powder, and sprinkle on shrimp.

Prepare the grill. Place the grill screen on the grill and allow to get hot. Spread shrimp evenly over the screen and cook 6–8 minutes, turning once.

Wrap the tortillas in aluminum foil in groups of three. Warm the foil packages on the grill 4–5 minutes, turning once.

Combine the shredded lettuce and cabbages.

To serve, give each person a package of tortillas. Place 3 shrimp in each tortilla, and fill with shredded cabbage mixture. Add Fresh Fruit Pico de Gallo and Jalapeño and Roasted Garlic Crème Fraîche to taste.

YIELD: 18 tacos

# Fresh Fruit Pico de Gallo

1 cup small dice tomatoes

¼ cup thinly sliced green
onions

2 Tbl chopped cilantro

2 tsp minced fresh jalapeños,
seeds removed

½ cup small dice pineapple

1 kiwi, peeled, small dice

½ cup small dice peeled fresh
peaches

½ cup orange segments

½ cup lime segments

½ tsp salt

Combine all ingredients together and refrigerate until ready
to serve.

YIELD: 3 cups

# Jalapeño and Roasted Garlic Crème Fraîche

1 cup heavy whipping cream

2 tsp lemon juice

¼ cup sour cream

1 Tbl finely chopped canned
jalapeños

¼ cup Roasted Garlic Puree
(page 42)

½ tsp salt

Combine heavy whipping cream and lemon juice in an airtight
container and put it in a warm place 6–8 hours. (It should reach
85–95 degrees.) Remove the cover and stir well. Refrigerate
overnight.

After the crème fraîche has set, stir in the sour cream, jalapeños,
roasted garlic, and salt. Store refrigerated until ready to serve.

YIELD: 1½ cups

# Bacon Cheeseburger Quesadillas

A great use for leftover burgers.

1 lb ground beef

¼ cup No-stick Grilling
    Marinade for Beef
    (page 205)

1 Tbl Steak Seasoning
    (page 211)

½ pound bacon, small dice

1½ cups small dice yellow
    onions

1 tsp kosher salt

1 tsp freshly ground black
    pepper

2 cups shredded cheddar
    cheese

1½ cups shredded pepperjack
    cheese

Eight 10-inch flour tortillas

¼ cup olive oil

Sour cream and salsa for
    serving

Make 4 hamburger patties using the ground beef. Brush each patty with the no-stick marinade and allow to marinate 30 minutes. Sprinkle each patty with steak seasoning.

Prepare the grill. Cook the burgers on direct high heat to medium well, approximately 14 minutes.

While burgers are cooking, place the diced bacon in a large sauté pan over medium heat. Cook the bacon until it becomes brown and crispy, stirring often. Once the bacon is crisp, use a slotted spoon to remove from pan. Pour off most of the bacon fat, leaving just enough to coat the bottom of the pan. Place the diced onions, salt, and pepper in the hot bacon fat. Cook 6–7 minutes, stirring often.

Allow the bacon, onions, and hamburgers to cool completely.

Place the cooked burgers in the bowl of a food processor and pulse 6–7 times. The meat should be broken up but not ground fine.

Place the ground hamburger, onions, and bacon in a large mixing bowl and mix well. Blend in the shredded cheeses.

Lay the flour tortillas on a flat surface and divide the filling evenly among them. Spread the filling so that it covers one half of each tortilla. Fold the filled tortillas in half to form a semicircle.

Prepare the grill. Brush the tortillas with olive oil. Grill the quesadillas over direct medium heat until well marked, about 4–6 minutes on each side. Rotate the quesadillas while cooking to prevent burning. Remove the quesadillas from the grill and cut them into 4–6 triangles. Serve with sour cream and salsa.

**YIELD: 6–10 servings**

# Shrimp and Mushroom Quesadillas

The possibilities with this dish are only as limited as your imagination. Goat cheese or smoked cheddar, a flavored tortilla, or using a mix of mushrooms will change the flavor profile of the dish completely. Feel free to improvise.

¼ cup olive oil

1 lb fresh shrimp, small

1 tsp Old Bay seasoning

1 tsp crushed red pepper

2 cups thinly sliced mushrooms

¾ cup small dice yellow onions

¼ cup small dice red bell peppers

1 Tbl minced garlic

1 tsp Creole Seasoning (page 212)

1 tsp freshly ground black pepper

½ cup finely chopped green onions

¼ cup Pesto (page 21)

1½ cups shredded cheddar cheese

1 cup shredded mozzarella cheese

Six 8–10 inch flour tortillas

Sour cream and salsa for serving

Heat 2 tablespoons of the olive oil in a large sauté pan over high heat. Season the shrimp with the Old Bay seasoning. Place shrimp in the oil and cook 3 minutes. Add crushed red pepper, sliced mushrooms, diced onions and red bell peppers. Cook 6–7 minutes more. Add garlic, Creole Seasoning, and black pepper. Cook for 2 minutes more. Remove from heat and stir in the green onions. Allow mixture to cool completely.

Once the quesadilla filling is cool, add the pesto and shredded cheese; blend well.

Lay the flour tortillas on a flat surface and divide the filling evenly among them. Spread filling to cover one half of each tortilla. Fold the tortillas in half to form a semicircle.

Prepare the grill. Using a pastry brush, lightly coat the two sides of the quesadilla with the remaining olive oil. Grill the quesadillas over direct medium heat until well marked, 4–6 minutes on each side. Rotate the quesadillas while cooking to prevent burning. Remove the quesadillas from the grill and cut them into 4–6 triangles. Serve with sour cream and salsa.

YIELD: 6–10 servings

# Crawfish Quesadillas

We've been selling these in the Crescent City Grill for 20 years.
They are always crowd-pleasers.

¼ cup olive oil

¼ cup finely chopped green
    bell peppers

¼ cup finely chopped red
    bell peppers

1 jalapeño, small dice

½ cup finely chopped yellow
    onions

½ cup finely chopped green
    onions

1 Tbl minced garlic

2 tsp Creole Seasoning
    (page 212)

¾ lb crawfish tail meat, in
    whole pieces

2 Tbl chopped fresh cilantro

2½ cups shredded jalapeño
    Jack cheese

Six 8–10-inch flour tortillas

Sour cream and salsa for
    serving

In a large skillet, heat 2 tablespoons of the olive oil and sauté green bell peppers, red bell peppers, jalapeño, yellow onions, green onions, and garlic until tender. Remove from heat and add Creole seasoning and crawfish. Allow mixture to cool. Once cooled, add cilantro and cheese. Mix well.

Lay the flour tortillas on a flat surface and divide the filling evenly among them. Spread the filling so that it covers half of each tortilla. Fold the filled tortillas in half to form a semicircle.

Prepare the grill. Using a pastry brush, lightly coat both sides of the quesadilla with the remaining olive oil. Grill the quesadillas over direct medium heat until well marked, 4–6 minutes on each side. Rotate the quesadillas while cooking to prevent burning. Remove the quesadillas from the grill and cut them into 4–6 triangles. Serve with sour cream and salsa.

YIELD: 6–10 servings

# Chicken Pesto Quesadillas

I love pesto sauce. Canned pimientos are a poor substitution for roasted red bell peppers.
*huh?* Roasting red bell peppers is easy; no kitchen should be without a supply in the fridge.

¼ cup olive oil

2 cups thinly sliced
mushrooms

1 cup small dice yellow onions

1 Tbl minced Garlic

1 tsp Creole Seasoning
(page 212)

1 tsp freshly ground black
pepper

½ cup finely chopped green
onions

½ cup Pesto (page 21)

¾ lb small dice grilled chicken

1½ cups shredded jalapeño
Jack cheese

1 cup shredded mozzarella
cheese

Six 8–10-inch flour tortillas

Sour cream and salsa for
serving

Heat 2 tablespoons of the olive oil over high heat in a large sauté pan. When the oil becomes very hot, add mushrooms to the pan. Cook 1 minute without moving the mushrooms at all. Stir mushrooms after the first minute, and cook 1 more minute. Add the diced onions, garlic, Creole Seasoning, and black pepper, and cook 5 more minutes, until the onions are tender and the moisture from the mushrooms has cooked out. Remove from the heat and place in a mixing bowl. Stir in the green onions, Pesto, and chicken, and allow mixture to cool completely. Add the shredded cheese.

Lay the flour tortillas on a flat surface and divide the filling evenly among them. Spread the filling so that it covers half of each tortilla. Fold tortillas in half to form a semicircle.

Prepare the grill. Using a pastry brush, lightly coat both sides of the quesadillas with the remaining olive oil. Grill the quesadillas over direct medium heat until well marked, 4–6 minutes on each side. Rotate the quesadillas while cooking to prevent burning. Remove the quesadillas from the grill and cut them into 4–6 triangles. Serve with sour cream and salsa.

YIELD: 6–10 servings

# Pesto

½ bunch parsley leaves, stems removed

1 bunch basil leaves, stems removed

1 cup grated Parmesan cheese, good quality

8 cloves garlic, minced

1 cup pine nuts, chopped

1 cup extra virgin olive oil

Place all ingredients except olive oil in a food processor. Process until smooth. With machine running, slowly add oil. Turn off the processor and scrape down the sides. Continue to process until you have a smooth paste. Refrigerate until needed, up to 1 week. Pesto freezes well.

YIELD: 2½ cups

# Grilled Crawfish Pizza

A dish I developed years ago and which is still a crowd-pleaser. The Basil Tapenade is great on its own as a dip for toasted pita chips or spreading on focaccia. If you can't purchase fresh crawfish in your area, feel free to substitute shrimp.

1 Tbl olive oil

½ cup finely chopped green bell peppers

½ cup finely chopped yellow onions

½ cup finely chopped green onions

1 Tbl minced garlic

2 tsp Creole Seasoning (page 212)

¾ lb crawfish tail meat, cooked and in whole pieces

1½ cups Basil Tapenade (page 24)

6 Pizza Crusts (page 24)

1½ cups shredded mozzarella cheese

1 cup shredded jalapeño Jack cheese

½ cup freshly grated Parmesan cheese

In a large skillet, heat olive oil over medium heat. Sauté peppers, onions, and garlic until slightly tender. Add Creole Seasoning and crawfish. Remove from heat and let cool slightly (may be prepared a day in advance).

Spread the Basil Tapenade evenly on top of each prepared pizza crust. Distribute the crawfish mixture over the tapenade. Combine the cheeses together. Top each pizza with the cheese mixture.

Prepare the grill. Cook the pizzas over indirect medium heat, covered, until the topping is hot and the cheeses have melted.

Allow the pizzas to cool slightly before cutting.

YIELD: 6–10 servings

(continued)

# Basil Tapenade

1 cup black olives

1½ ounces anchovies, drained and patted dry

1 tsp Dijon mustard

2 Tbl capers

2 Tbl freshly squeezed lemon juice

2 Tbl brandy

3 Tbl olive oil

½ tsp freshly ground black pepper

1 cup Pesto (p. 21)

½ of 10-ounce can Rotel tomatoes, drained

Blend the black olives, anchovies, Dijon, capers, lemon juice, and brandy in a food processor until the mixture begins to get smooth. Slowly add olive oil and pepper. Add pesto and tomatoes, and pulse until all ingredients are incorporated into a smooth, spreadable sauce. May be made and stored in refrigerator for up to 1 week.

YIELD: 3 cups

# Pizza Crusts

2 packages active dry yeast

1 tsp sugar

2 tsp honey

1½ cups warm water

5¼ cups all-purpose flour

1 Tbl salt

¼ cup olive oil, plus additional olive oil for brushing the pizza dough

Dissolve yeast, sugar, and honey in ½ cup of warm water.

Using a mixer with a dough hook, place flour and salt in bowl and mix thoroughly. On low speed, slowly drizzle in oil and continue to mix until evenly distributed. Next, add dissolved yeast. Add remaining cup of water. Once the dough begins to come together, continue kneading on low speed for 5 minutes.

Transfer the dough onto a floured surface and work it by hand for 3–4 more minutes. The dough should now be smooth and slightly firm and dry. Place the dough in a large bowl, cover it with a damp towel, and place it in a warm place to rise for ½ hour.

*"The Basil Tapenade is great on its own as a dip for toasted pita chips or spreading on focaccia."*

Divide the dough into six 6-ounce sections. On a dry surface, work each individual ball by rotating it in a circular motion, continually tucking the sides down and under. Form dough into a smooth ball with no air pockets. Place the balls on a slightly oiled baking sheet and cover for 30 minutes. This may be done 1–2 days in advance. Dough balls can be covered tightly with plastic and kept in refrigerator.

To stretch the dough, sprinkle a smooth surface with flour or cornmeal and flatten the dough to about 2 inches thick. Then begin gently pulling the sides and rotating the dough in a circular motion, slowly stretching it. You should be able to stretch the dough to a 7-inch diameter. Lightly brush the dough with oil and grill on direct medium heat until they are marked on the underside, about 2–3 minutes. Rotate the dough once or twice to prevent burning. Turn the dough over and cook for 2–3 more minutes. Remove the dough from the grill.

At this point in time you can either top the pizzas and finish the cooking process in an oven or over indirect medium heat, or allow them to cool and store individually wrapped in the refrigerator or freezer until needed.

**YIELD: Six 7-inch crusts**

# Grilled BBQ Chicken Pizza

A true Southern twist on a tried and true classic.

1 Tbl olive oil

1 cup julienned yellow onions

1 tsp kosher salt

½ tsp freshly ground black
  pepper

1 Tbl minced garlic

¾ lb fully cooked grilled
  chicken, small dice

1 cup BBQ sauce

6 Pizza Crusts, prepared and
  pre-grilled (page 24)

2½ cups mozzarella cheese

1 cup roasted red bell peppers,
  cut into long strips

In a large skillet, heat olive oil over medium heat. Place the onions, salt, and pepper in the heated oil and lower the heat. Cook 12–15 minutes, stirring often. Onions should caramelize and become brown, but not burn. Add the garlic and cook 3 minutes more.

Combine the onion mixture, chicken, and half of the BBQ sauce in a mixing bowl. Brush the remaining barbeque sauce on the top of each prepared pizza crust. Distribute the chicken mixture over the barbeque sauce. Top each pizza with the cheese. Divide the roasted bell pepper strips over the top of the cheese.

Prepare the grill. Cook the pizzas, covered, over indirect medium heat or in a 400-degree oven until the topping is hot and the cheese has melted.

Allow the pizzas to cool slightly before cutting.

YIELD: 6 servings

# Grilled Shrimp and Pesto Pizzas

Be careful not to burn the crusts. As with tortillas, pizza crusts are sensitive to flames and will char in seconds. Freshly grated Parmesan is a must—never use the powdered stuff that comes in a can.

4 Tbl olive oil

¾ lb fresh shrimp, small

1 tsp Old Bay seasoning

2 tsp freshly ground black pepper

1 Tbl minced garlic

1½ cups button mushrooms, thin sliced

½ cup finely chopped red bell peppers

½ cup finely chopped red onions

½ cup finely chopped green onions

6 Pizza Crusts, prepared and pre-grilled (page 24)

1½ cups fresh Pesto (page 21)

1½ cups shredded mozzarella cheese

1 cup shredded jalapeño Jack cheese

¾ cup shredded cheddar cheese

½ cup freshly grated Parmesan cheese

In a large skillet, heat olive oil over medium heat. Season the shrimp with the Old Bay seasoning and black pepper, and cook for 2 minutes. Add the garlic, mushrooms, peppers, and red onions, and cook for 6–8 more minutes. Remove from heat and stir in the green onions. Cool slightly (may be prepared a day in advance).

Spread the pesto evenly on top of each prepared pizza crust. Distribute the shrimp mixture over the pesto. Combine the cheeses. Top each pizza with the cheese mixture. Continue to cook the pizzas over indirect medium heat or in a 400-degree oven until the topping is hot and the cheeses have melted.

Allow the pizzas to cool slightly before cutting.

YIELD: 6–10 servings

# Chicken Skewers

If you don't use wooden skewers, you'll miss out on a world of flavor. Plan ahead and take the extra time to soak your wooden skewers; you won't regret it. Already butchered, pre-portioned chicken tenders work well and save time.

**SKEWER SOAK**

1 cup water

1 Tbl soy sauce

¼ cup coconut milk

Twenty-four 6-inch wooden skewers

**CHICKEN MARINADE**

1 ¼ lbs boneless, skinless chicken breasts, cut into 24 strips

¼ cup pineapple juice

2 Tbl soy sauce

1 tsp minced garlic

1 Tbl sesame oil

¼ cup Thai chili sauce

2–3 Tbl peanut oil

**FOR THE SKEWERS:** Combine water, soy sauce, and coconut milk together and soak the skewers in the mixture for 2–4 hours. Use a plastic-wrapped weight to keep the skewers submerged in the mixture.

**FOR THE CHICKEN:** Thread chicken onto the soaked skewers, leaving a small portion of the skewer empty so it can be picked up after cooking.

Combine pineapple juice, soy sauce, garlic, sesame oil, and chili sauce.

Pour marinade over the chicken skewers and allow to soak for 3–4 hours. The chicken should be refrigerated while marinating.

Drain the marinated skewers and pat dry with paper towels. Take small squares of aluminum foil and wrap the exposed wooden skewers. Using a pastry brush, coat chicken skewers with the peanut oil.

Prepare the grill. Cook the skewers over direct high heat for 5–7 minutes, turning once while cooking. Remove the foil from the ends of the skewers and arrange on a serving dish. Drizzle with Dipping Sauce (recipe follows), or serve it on the side.

**YIELD: 6–8 servings**

(continued)

# Dipping Sauce

2 Tbl peanut oil

1 cup unsalted peanuts

1 Tbl minced shallots

1 Tbl minced ginger

2 cloves minced garlic

2 tsp fresh minced jalapeños

½ cup coconut milk

¼ cup rice vinegar

¼ cup cottonseed oil

¼ cup warm water

2 Tbl soy sauce

1 lime, juiced

½ tsp lime zest

2 Tbl chopped fresh cilantro

½ tsp salt

¼ tsp cayenne pepper

In a skillet heat 1 tablespoon of the peanut oil and sauté the peanuts to golden brown, 4–6 minutes. Drain peanuts on paper towels.

Heat the remaining peanut oil and cook shallots, ginger, garlic, and jalapeños over low heat 4–5 minutes. Add the coconut milk and vinegar and simmer slowly 5 minutes.

Place peanuts into the simmering liquid and continue to cook 5 minutes. Remove from heat and allow to cool 10 minutes.

Transfer mixture to a blender and puree until smooth. Continue to blend, adding in remaining ingredients. (If the sauce is too thick, add a bit more warm water.)

The sauce may be made several days in advance. Store in an air-tight container in the refrigerator. Best when served at room temperature.

YIELD: 3 cups

# Grilled Hot Wings

These take time, but they're worth it. Make a batch for your guests, and make another batch to eat once they leave.

1 gallon water

⅓ cup soy sauce

¼ cup sugar

2 Tbl kosher salt

2 Tbl crushed red pepper flakes

½ cup white vinegar

3 lbs fresh chicken wings

1½ cup Louisiana hot sauce

½ cup melted butter

½ cup honey

Blue Cheese Dressing
    (page 33)

In a large stockpot, combine the water, soy sauce, sugar, salt, red pepper flakes, and vinegar. Bring this mixture to a simmer, and allow it to cook for 10 minutes. Place the chicken wings into the simmering mixture. Once the water returns to simmer, cook the wings for 30 minutes.

Using a large colander, strain and discard the liquid. Allow the chicken wings to cool in the refrigerator for 1 hour. This step may be done 1–2 days in advance.

Combine the hot sauce, melted butter, and honey in a mixing bowl. Toss the wings in the sauce and remove them using a slotted spoon; reserve sauce.

Spread the wings out evenly on the grill over direct medium heat. Cook 30–40 minutes. Every 15 minutes, place the wings back in the sauce to coat the surface, and then return them to the grill.

Remove from the grill and serve with Blue Cheese Dressing for dipping.

YIELD: 8–10 servings

# Blue Cheese Dressing

1 cup mayonnaise

½ cup crumbled blue cheese

⅓ cup sour cream

¾ cup half-and-half

½ tsp paprika

1 Tbl garlic powder

1 tsp Worcestershire sauce

½ tsp white pepper

In a large stainless steel bowl, combine the mayonnaise, blue cheese, sour cream, and half-and-half with a wire whisk. Mix thoroughly. Add the remaining ingredients and blend well. Refrigerate until needed. This dressing is better if it is made a day in advance.

YIELD: 2½ cups

# BBQ Oysters

Make sure not to overcook the oysters or they'll be dry and rubbery.

1 Tbl bacon fat

2 tsp minced yellow onions

2 tsp minced fresh jalapeños

1 tsp minced garlic

¼ tsp kosher salt

¼ tsp freshly ground black
   pepper

2 Tbl tomato paste

¼ cup balsamic vinegar

½ tsp yellow mustard

¼ cup ketchup

¼ cup hoisin sauce

1 Tbl soy sauce

24 fresh oysters

Heat the bacon fat in a small sauce pot over low heat. Cook the onions, jalapeños, garlic, salt, and pepper for 3–4 minutes. Turn heat to medium and add tomato paste. Cook 4–5 minutes, stirring constantly. Add remaining ingredients except oysters, and simmer for 10–15 minutes, stirring occasionally.

Using a kitchen towel, hold each oyster firmly. Insert an oyster knife in the small opening between the shells where the oyster is hinged. Gently pry open the oyster. Loosen the oyster from the shell by carefully running the knife below the oyster, keeping the oyster liquor in the shell. Discard the top shell.

Top each oyster with a heaping teaspoon of the sauce.

Prepare the grill. Grill the oysters, shell side down, over direct high heat for 4–5 minutes. Use tongs to remove the oysters from the grill and serve immediately.

YIELD: **4–8 servings**

# Yellowfin Tuna Kabobs

Ahi, bluefin, and all fresh varieties of tuna work well here. Great for a summer party by the pool.

1 Tbl sesame seed oil

¼ cup vegetable oil

¼ cup soy sauce

2 Tbl orange juice

1 Tbl honey

1 Tbl dry ginger

1 Tbl minced garlic

2 lbs fresh yellowfin tuna, cut into 3–4 thick steaks

1 cup wood chips, soaked in water for 1 hour

12 medium button mushrooms, cut in half

1 red onion, peeled and cut into 1½-inch squares

12 pineapple chunks

1 red bell pepper, cut into twelve 1-inch squares

2 Tbl olive oil

2 tsp kosher salt

1 tsp freshly ground black pepper

Mix together the sesame oil, vegetable oil, soy sauce, orange juice, honey, ginger, and garlic, and blend well. Place the tuna and marinade into a large baggie. Seal the baggie and refrigerate for 1 hour.

Prepare the smoker for indirect VERY LOW heat. Place the marinated tuna as far from the heat as possible and place a small handful of chips on the coals. Smoke the tuna 30–40 minutes, making sure that the tuna does not cook. Remove the tuna from the smoker and refrigerate 1 hour.

Once the tuna has chilled completely, cut the steaks into 1½–2-inch cubes.

Using 12 skewers, alternately skewer the tuna with the vegetables. Each skewer should have 2 pieces of mushrooms, 2 pieces of onion, 1 pineapple chunk, and 1 bell pepper piece, along with the tuna.

Prepare the grill. Brush the skewers with olive oil, and season with salt and pepper. Grill over direct high heat for 5–7 minutes, turning once. Use the remaining marinade to brush the skewers while cooking.

YIELD: 6 servings

# Grilled Oysters Rockefeller

A twist on the tried-and-true New Orleans classic. This is a less anise-flavored version; I prefer the flavor profile here to the original.

1 cup unsalted butter

2 Tbl minced garlic

1 tsp dried tarragon

1 ½ cups panko bread crumbs

½ cup small dice shallots

8 cups chopped fresh spinach

1 cup Pernod

1 tsp kosher salt

½ tsp freshly ground black
    pepper

½ tsp hot sauce

⅓ cup olive oil

1 cup grated Parmesan cheese

3 Tbl chopped parsley

24 fresh oysters

Melt butter in a skillet. Sauté the garlic and dried tarragon for 2 minutes. Take half of the garlic butter and add it to the bread crumbs in a mixing bowl. Set aside to cool.

To the remaining garlic butter in the skillet, add the shallots and spinach, and cook 3 minutes, until the spinach wilts. Deglaze the pan with Pernod. Season with salt and pepper and hot sauce. Allow the mixture to cook for a few minutes.

To the bread crumbs, add the olive oil, Parmesan, and parsley, and season with salt and pepper to taste.

Using a kitchen towel, hold each oyster firmly. Insert an oyster knife in the small opening between the shells where the oyster is hinged. Gently pry open the oyster. Loosen the oyster from the shell by carefully running the knife below the oyster, trying to keep as much of the oyster liquor in place.

Top each oyster with 2 teaspoons of the spinach mixture. Sprinkle the spinach with the prepared bread crumbs.

Prepare the grill. Cook the oysters, shell side down, over direct high heat for 5–6 minutes. Use tongs to remove the oysters from the grill and serve immediately.

YIELD: 4–8 servings, depending on how much you or your guests like oysters

# Grilled Garlic-Romano Oysters

This recipe shows up in many variations all throughout New Orleans. If you have a friend who knows how to shuck oysters, put him to work and keep the grill full.

1 lb unsalted butter

1 Tbl minced fresh garlic

24 fresh oysters

½ cup freshly grated Romano cheese

½ tsp freshly ground black pepper

1 small loaf French bread

Place the butter in a small sauce pot over medium high heat and bring to a simmer. Use a ladle to skim off the light-colored foam that rises to the top. The butter will become clear and yellow. As soon as the butter is clear, turn the heat to low and add the minced garlic. Cook for 1 more minute and remove the butter from the heat.

Using a kitchen towel, hold each oyster firmly. Insert an oyster knife in the small opening between the shells where the oyster is hinged. Gently pry open the oyster. Loosen the oyster from the shell by carefully running the knife below the oyster, keeping as much of the oyster liquor in place.

Prepare the grill. Place the oysters on direct high heat and sprinkle each one with 1 teaspoon of Romano cheese. Cook until the cheese begins to brown, about 3 minutes. Drizzle 1–2 teaspoons of butter over each oyster and cook for 1–2 more minutes. Remove the oysters from the heat and add the freshly ground black pepper.

Wrap the French bread in aluminum foil and warm it with indirect high heat, cooking for 10–12 minutes, turning once while cooking. Slice just before serving.

Serve the oysters immediately with the warmed French bread and the remaining garlic butter on the side.

YIELD: 4–8 servings

# Grilled Roasted Garlic-Lemon Pepper Oysters

Roasting garlic mellows the pungency. Take the time to follow the simple garlic-roasting recipe and keep extra in your refrigerator. If you don't have a pastry bag to pipe the butter, roll the softened butter in parchment or waxed paper as you would a compound butter, freeze solid, and slice disks of the butter.

¼ cup olive oil

1 Tbl minced shallots

½ cup Roasted Garlic Puree (recipe follows)

1 tsp kosher salt

2 Tbl white wine

2 tsp lemon pepper seasoning

2 Tbl finely chopped parsley

1 cup unsalted butter, softened

2 tsp freshly squeezed lemon juice

1 tsp Worcestershire sauce

1 tsp hot sauce

24 fresh oysters

In a small sauté pan, heat the oil over low heat. Cook the shallots, garlic puree, and salt for 2–3 minutes. Add the wine, lemon pepper, and parsley and cook 3 minutes more, stirring often. Remove from heat and cool completely.

Place softened butter in a mixing bowl. Add lemon juice, Worcestershire, and hot sauce. Using a rubber spatula, blend together with the garlic puree. Place the butter in a pastry bag with a medium star tip attached.

Line a baking sheet with waxed paper. Pipe butter rosettes, 1½–2 teaspoons in size, onto the waxed paper. You should have 24 rosettes when finished. Refrigerate until needed.

Using a kitchen towel, hold each oyster firmly. Insert an oyster knife in the small opening between the shells where the oyster is hinged. Gently pry open the oyster. Keep the oyster liquor in place.

Prepare the grill. Cook the oysters, shell side down, over direct high heat for 4–5 minutes. Use tongs to remove the oysters from the grill, and top each one with a rosette of the butter.

Serve immediately.

YIELD: 4–8 servings

(continued)

# Roasted Garlic Puree

**3 whole heads of garlic**

**¼ cup olive oil**

**2 tsp kosher salt**

Preheat oven to 350°.

Remove the outermost layers of the skin on the garlic heads. Cut the top off so that the garlic cloves are exposed and place them in a shallow baking dish. Heat the olive oil over high heat for 1–2 minutes. Stir the salt into the oil and pour the oil directly over the tops of the garlic. Cover the garlic with foil and bake for 30 minutes. Remove the foil and bake for an additional 8 minutes.

Remove from the oven and cool the garlic. To remove the roasted garlic cloves, gently squeeze the bottom of the head and the garlic should come out easily.

Place the roasted garlic cloves on a cutting board and, using the flat side of a chef's knife, smash the garlic into a puree.

**YIELD: ⅓–½ cup garlic puree**

*"Roasting garlic mellows the pungency. Take the time to follow the simple garlic-roasting recipe and keep extra in your refrigerator."*

# Three-Layered Grilled Shrimp Caesar Salad

A popular lunch feature in the Crescent City Grill. Make all of the components in advance and compose the salad just before serving. This dish can be served on a platter or in a trifle dish to show off the layers.

Caesar Salad
   (recipe follows)

Garlic Croutons
   (recipe follows)

Pasta Salad
   (recipe follows)

Grilled Shrimp
   (recipe follows)

TO ASSEMBLE: Arrange the prepared Caesar Salad on a serving platter. Next, place the Pasta Salad atop the Caesar Salad. Finally, top the pasta with the Grilled Shrimp and serve immediately.

YIELD: 6 servings

(continued)

# Caesar Salad

**DRESSING**

2 egg yolks

¼ cup fresh lemon juice

2 Tbl minced garlic

3 anchovies

2 Tbl red wine vinegar

1 Tbl Worcestershire sauce

2 Tbl Dijon mustard

1 cup light olive oil

3 romaine hearts or 1 large head of romaine (outer leaves discarded)

2 cups Garlic Croutons (recipe follows)

1½ cups Caesar Salad Dressing

½ cup freshly grated Parmesan cheese

**FOR THE DRESSING:** Combine egg yolks, lemon juice, garlic, anchovies, vinegar, Worcestershire sauce, and Dijon mustard in a food processor. Puree for 1–2 minutes. With processor running, slowly drizzle in olive oil. If the mixture becomes too thick, add 1–2 tablespoons of warm water, and continue to add the oil. Store refrigerated until ready to use.

**YIELD: 2 cups**

**FOR THE SALAD:** Cut the lettuce into bite-sized pieces. Wash and dry the lettuce well. Place lettuce in a large mixing bowl, add croutons and just enough dressing to wet, and mix well.

**YIELD: 6 salads**

# Garlic Croutons

2 cups French bread cut into ½-inch cubes

3 Tbl olive oil

2 tsp garlic powder

½ tsp kosher salt

Preheat oven to 250°.

In a large stainless steel bowl, toss the French bread with the olive oil, garlic powder, and salt. Place on a baking sheet and bake 30–45 minutes until crispy.

# Pasta Salad

½ lb rotini pasta

1½ cups small dice fresh
   tomatoes

¾ cup sliced black olives

½ cup thinly sliced green
   onions

DRESSING

½ cup fresh Pesto (page 21)

¼ cup sour cream

½ cup mayonnaise

¼ cup half-and-half

½ tsp Poultry Seasoning
   (page 213)

1 tsp freshly ground black
   pepper

½ tsp kosher salt

Cook the pasta, following the manufacturer's directions on the package. Once cooked, cool the pasta thoroughly by soaking in ice water. Add tomato, black olives, and green onions to the pasta. Prepare the dressing by combining all ingredients and mixing well. Toss chilled pasta with the salad dressing.

# Grilled Shrimp

2 lbs small shrimp

⅓ cup shrimp nonstick grilling
   marinade

1 tsp freshly ground black
   pepper

1 tsp Old Bay seasoning

Use a grill screen or skewers so that the shrimp don't fall right through the grill.

Coat shrimp with the marinade and refrigerate 1 hour.

Sprinkle shrimp with black pepper and Old Bay seasoning.

Prepare the grill for direct-high-heat cooking. Place grill screen on the prepared grill. Spread shrimp evenly on the screen and cook 5–7 minutes, turning once.

*"People underestimate the value of a good hamburger bun. Buy the best you can find—it will make a huge difference."*

# Burgers and Sandwiches

# Mushroom-Swiss Burgers with Dijon-Horseradish Sauce

People underestimate the value of a good hamburger bun. Buy the best you can find—it will make a huge difference. When grilling burgers, I always grill a few extra and, once cooked, let them cool slightly and place them immediately in Ziploc bags, then in the freezer. Weeks later—when defrosted slowly in a microwave—they taste as if they have just come off of the grill.

3 lbs ground beef

⅓ cup No-stick Grilling Marinade for Beef (page 205)

1 Tbl Steak Seasoning (page 211)

2 Tbl unsalted butter

3 cups sliced mushrooms

1 tsp salt

1 tsp freshly ground black pepper

Six 1-ounce slices Swiss cheese

6 hamburger buns

¼ cup melted unsalted butter

1 recipe Dijon-Horseradish Sauce (page 228)

1½ cups fresh spinach leaves

6 red onion slices

Divide the ground beef into six equal parts and form burger patties, approximately 1½ inches thick.

Prepare the grill: Brush the surface of the burgers with the no-stick marinade and sprinkle with the steak seasoning. Cook over direct high heat for 8–10 minutes.

While the burgers are cooking:

Heat the butter in a medium sauté pan over high heat. Place mushrooms, salt, and pepper in the hot butter and sauté mushrooms for 6–7 minutes, stirring occasionally. Drain excess liquid.

While they are still on the grill, top each burger with one slice of cheese. Divide the mushrooms evenly and place them atop the cheese. Close the lid on the grill and cook just until the cheese melts.

Brush the hamburger buns with the melted butter and toast on the grill over medium direct heat for 2–3 minutes.

Spread the Dijon-Horseradish Sauce on both sides of the bun. Place a burger on each bun and top with the fresh spinach leaves and red onions.

YIELD: 6 hamburgers

# Black and Blue Burger

My wife loves blue cheese. These are her favorite burgers. Experiment with different varieties of blue-veined cheeses such as Gorgonzola or Stilton.

3 lbs ground beef

⅓ cup blackening seasoning

1 Tbl kosher salt

½ pound blue cheese crumbles

6 hamburger buns

¼ cup melted unsalted butter

6 slices red onions

8–12 slices ripe tomatoes

2 cups shredded iceberg lettuce

1 recipe Blue Cheese Dressing
    (page 33)

Divide the ground beef into 6 equal parts and form 1½-inch-thick patties.

Sprinkle patties with the blackening seasoning and salt. Cook over direct high heat for 8–10 minutes for medium–medium well burgers (155–160 degrees). While the burgers are still on the grill, top with blue cheese crumbles, dividing equally between burgers. Close the grill lid to melt blue cheese.

Brush the inside surfaces of the hamburger buns with the melted butter. Place on grill and cook over medium direct heat for 2–3 minutes. Place burgers on the grilled buns and top with onions, tomatoes, and lettuce. Serve the blue cheese dressing on the side.

YIELD: 6 burgers

# Cracked-Pepper Burgers with Mustard Cognac Sauce

Leaner ground beef might be healthier, but I never use any ground beef with less than 20 percent fat content. Skip dessert if you have to, but never use extra-lean ground beef.

3 lbs ground beef

1 recipe Mustard Cognac Sauce (page 157)

2 tsp Steak Seasoning (page 211)

⅓–½ cup cracked black peppercorns

6 kaiser rolls

6–8 leaves romaine lettuce

8–10 slices ripe tomatoes

Dijon mustard for serving

Divide the ground beef into 6 equal parts and form burger patties, about 1½ inches in thickness.

Divide the Mustard Cognac Sauce in half. Use a pastry brush to coat the surface of the hamburger patties with the Mustard Cognac Sauce. Sprinkle the patties with the Steak Seasoning. Firmly press the cracked black peppercorns onto the hamburger patties.

Prepare grill. Cook over direct high heat for 8–10 minutes.

Brush the inside surfaces of the kaiser rolls with the remaining Mustard Cognac Sauce. Grill over medium direct heat for 2–3 minutes. Place the burgers on the grilled rolls and top with the sliced tomatoes and a lettuce leaf. Serve with Dijon mustard on the side.

YIELD: 6 great burgers

# Smoked Eye of Round Sandwich

Growing up, my family always took a marinated eye of round to the beach on vacation. When kept in a refrigerator at the beach, the cool meat is perfect for a lunch out of the hot sun. Good luck trying to decide which sauce to use. Better yet, make two sandwiches and use both.

1 eye of round roast, about 2½ lbs

¼ cup No-stick Grilling Marinade for Beef (page 205)

1 Tbl Creole Seasoning (page 212)

1 Tbl freshly ground black pepper

6–8 hamburger buns

¼ cup olive oil

1 recipe Tobacco Onions (page 91)

8–10 fresh tomato slices

1½ –2 cups shredded romaine lettuce

1 recipe Basil Aioli (page 111)

1 recipe Dijon-Horseradish Sauce (page 228)

Rub the no-stick marinade over the entire surface of the roast and marinate at room temperature for 1 hour before grilling. Sprinkle the surface of the roast with the Creole Seasoning and black pepper.

Prepare the grill. Sear the roast over direct high heat for 12–15 minutes, turning it every 3–4 minutes. Move the roast to indirect high heat and continue cooking until desired doneness is reached, 20–30 minutes more for medium (145 degrees).

Remove the roast from the grill and allow it to rest for 15 minutes before slicing. While the roast is resting, brush the inside surfaces of the hamburger buns with the olive oil. Grill for 2–3 minutes.

Slice the eye roast as thin as possible. Layer the bun with thin slices of the beef, and top with the tobacco onions, tomato slices, and romaine lettuce. Serve with Basil Aioli and Dijon-Horseradish Sauce on the side.

YIELD: 6–8 sandwiches

# Beef Tenderloin Sandwiches

Your friends will love you for making these. Great for summer suppers or cocktail parties when offered with a variety of breads and rolls.

1 cup Wish-Bone Italian dressing

¼ cup Worcestershire sauce

3 lbs whole beef tenderloin, cleaned and trimmed

2 Tbl Steak Seasoning (page 211)

24 small rolls, cut in half, crosswise

Combine the Italian dressing and Worcestershire sauce and rub the outside of the tenderloin. Marinate for 30–45 minutes.

Prepare the grill. Sprinkle the tenderloin with the Steak Seasoning. Sear the tenderloin over direct medium heat for 15 minutes. Turn it one quarter turn every 4–5 minutes during the searing process.

Move the tenderloin to cook over indirect heat and cook until desired doneness is reached, 20–30 minutes for medium rare (135 degrees). Turn the tenderloin once every 15 minutes during this stage. Remove the tenderloin from the grill and allow it to rest for 5–10 minutes before carving.

Slice into thin slices. Place 2–3 slices on a roll and top with one or more of the following sauces.

YIELD: **24 small sandwiches**

(continued)

All of the sauces may be made 3–4 days in advance, and stored
in the refrigerator until needed.

## Honey-spiked Dijon Mustard

½ cup Dijon mustard

2 Tbl yellow mustard

1 Tbl sour cream

2 Tbl mayonnaise

¼ cup honey

2 tsp chopped fresh parsley

1 tsp chopped fresh thyme
    leaves

½ tsp hot sauce

1 tsp balsamic vinegar

¼ tsp salt

Using a wire whisk, combine all ingredients together.
Store covered and refrigerated until ready to serve.

YIELD: 1¼ cups

## Horseradish Cream Cheese Spread

½ cup cream cheese, softened

¼ cup sour cream

2 Tbl mayonnaise

1 tsp Creole mustard

1 tsp freshly ground black
    pepper

⅓ cup prepared horseradish

2 Tbl minced red onions

¼ tsp minced fresh garlic

1 Tbl chopped fresh chives

1 Tbl chopped fresh parsley

½ tsp salt

Use a wire whisk to blend together the cream cheese,
sour cream, and mayonnaise. Mix until smooth. Add the
remaining ingredients and mix well.

YIELD: 1½ cups

# Roasted Garlic Mayonnaise

2 egg yolks

1 tsp kosher salt

1 tsp Dijon mustard

2 Tbl white vinegar

1 Tbl lemon juice

⅓ cup Roasted Garlic Puree
  (page 42)

1¼ cups canola oil

1 tsp freshly ground black
  pepper

Place the egg yolks, salt, and mustard in a food processor. Blend. Combine the vinegar and lemon juice together, and add half of the mixture to the food processor. Add the Roasted Garlic Puree. Slowly drizzle in the oil. As the mixture thickens, add the remaining vinegar and lemon juice. Add the black pepper. If the mayonnaise becomes too thick, use a small amount of warm water to thin it.

YIELD: 2 cups

*"Your friends will love you for making these. Great for summer suppers or cocktail parties when offered with a variety of breads and rolls."*

# Pork Tenderloin Po-Boy

Keep plenty of this dry rub on hand and use it whenever you're cooking pork chops or pork roast. Don't overcook your pork.

1 tsp paprika

1 tsp brown sugar

1 tsp kosher salt

1 tsp chili powder

1 tsp dry mustard

1 tsp freshly ground black pepper

¼ tsp ground cinnamon

1 tsp ground coriander

2 pork tenderloins, approximately 1 lb each, cleaned and trimmed

1–2 Tbl olive oil

Six 8-inch French bread or sourdough rolls, split down the middle

1 recipe Chutney Mayonnaise (page 59)

2 cups shredded green leaf lettuce

3 Roma tomatoes, thinly sliced

½ cup shaved red onions, paper thin

Combine the dry ingredients in a small mixing bowl; blend well.

Lightly brush the tenderloins with the olive oil and spread the dry spice mixture over the pork. Press the spice mixture firmly into the pork.

Prepare the grill and cook over direct medium heat until the pork is barely pink in the center, 15–20 minutes (155 degrees). Turn the pork 2–3 times while cooking.

Remove the pork from the grill and allow to rest 5–10 minutes. While the pork is resting, grill the po-boy bread for 1–2 minutes on each side.

Spread the Chutney Mayonnaise on the toasted bread. Slice the pork into one-eighth-inch-thick slices. Place several slices of pork on each roll and top with shredded lettuce, tomatoes, and red onion.

YIELD: 6 sandwiches

# Chutney Mayonnaise

1 Tbl olive oil

2 Tbl minced yellow onion

2 tsp minced garlic

¼ tsp salt

½ tsp curry powder

2 Tbl sherry

¾ cup chutney

¾ cup mayonnaise

In a small sauté pan, heat the olive oil over low heat. Place the onions, garlic, salt, and curry powder in the oil and cook for 1 minute. Add the sherry and cook until almost dry. Remove from heat and cool completely. Once the cooked mixture is cooled, combine it with the remaining ingredients. Store covered and refrigerated until ready to serve.

YIELD: 1½ cups

# Grilled Redfish Sandwiches with Seafood Rémoulade Sauce

Make Tobacco Onions at the last minute so they'll remain crispy. Grouper, red snapper, or trout can be substituted for the redfish; just purchase a mild-flavored variety and only use the freshest fish available. As with burgers, the bun makes a difference, so buy the best you can find. Raw red onions, thinly sliced, may be substituted for Tobacco Onions.

Six 6–7-oz redfish filets

¼ cup No-stick Grilling Marinade for Seafood (page 208)

1½ tsp Creole Seasoning (page 212)

6 hamburger buns

¼ cup olive oil

1 recipe Seafood Rémoulade (page 227)

1 Recipe Tobacco Onions (page 91)

1½ cups shredded green leaf lettuce

10–12 slices fresh tomatoes

Brush the fish filets with the No-stick Grilling Marinade and let sit for 1 hour. Sprinkle the filets with the Creole Seasoning and grill over direct high heat until the center of the fish is slightly pink, 6–8 minutes. Turn the filets once during cooking. Do not overcook.

Brush the inside surfaces of the hamburger buns with the olive oil. Grill over medium direct heat for 2–3 minutes.

To assemble the sandwiches, spread a small amount of the Seafood Rémoulade on the toasted surfaces of the hamburger buns. Place Tobacco Onions on the bottom bun, enough to cover the surface, then top with the fish, lettuce, tomatoes, and the top half of the bun.

Serve immediately.

YIELD: 6 sandwiches

# Big Easy Chicken Sandwiches

Experiment with different cheeses. Mushrooms can be made a few hours in advance and held warm. Caramelized Onions can be made a few days in advance and reheated. If you skip the bun and add veggies, you'll have a hearty entrée.

Six 5–6-oz boneless, skinless chicken breasts

½ cup No-stick Grilling Marinade for Poultry (page 206)

2 tsp Poultry Seasoning (page 213)

2 Tbl unsalted butter

3 cups sliced mushrooms

1 tsp kosher salt

1 tsp freshly ground black pepper

Six 1-ounce slices cheddar cheese

Six 1-ounce slices Monterey Jack cheese

1 recipe Caramelized Onions, hot (page 88)

6 hamburger buns

¼ cup melted unsalted butter

10–12 fresh tomato slices

Using a pastry brush, coat the chicken breasts with the marinade. Refrigerate for 30 minutes. Sprinkle the breasts with the Poultry Seasoning. Grill the chicken on direct high heat for 10–12 minutes, turning once during the grilling process.

While chicken is cooking: Heat butter in a medium sauté pan over high heat. Add mushrooms, salt, and pepper and sauté 6–7 minutes, stirring occasionally. Drain excess liquid.

Once the chicken has finished grilling, leave on the grill and top each chicken breast with 1 slice of each of the cheeses. Divide onions and mushrooms evenly among the chicken breasts and place atop the cheese. Close the grill lid and cook until the cheese has melted.

Brush the hamburger buns with melted butter and toast on the grill over medium direct heat for 2–3 minutes.

Place the chicken on the hamburger buns, top with the fresh tomato slices, and serve.

YIELD: 6 sandwiches

Cold Stuff

# Grilled Potato Salad

A grill screen works best when cooking the potatoes in this recipe. It's a great substitute for the traditional boiled potato salad. Yukon gold potatoes are a great substitution.

3 lbs red potatoes, cut into ¼-inch-thick circles

3 quarts water

1 Tbl kosher salt

½ cup No-stick Grilling Marinade for Vegetables (page 210)

1¼ cups mayonnaise

¼ cup yellow mustard

2 Tbl Dijon mustard

2 Tbl rice vinegar

1½ tsp freshly ground black pepper

2 tsp salt

1 cup chopped green onions

1 cup small dice red bell peppers

1 cup small dice celery

4 eggs, hard-boiled and chopped

¼ cup sweet pickle relish

Place the potatoes, water, and salt in a 6-quart pot. Cook over medium heat for 15 minutes. Do not let the water boil. Potatoes should be just less than fork-tender when they are removed from the water. Drain the par-cooked potatoes and allow to cool. Brush the cooled potatoes with the no-stick marinade.

Prepare the grill. Place the grill screen over direct medium heat. Spread the potatoes over the grill topper and cook 10–12 minutes, turning once while cooking. Remove the potatoes from the grill and allow to cool.

Combine the mayonnaise, mustards, vinegar, pepper, and salt to form a dressing. Gently fold in the potatoes and remaining ingredients into the dressing. Serve immediately.

If making in advance or eating leftovers, allow the potato salad to sit at room temperature for 20–30 minutes before serving.

YIELD: 2 quarts

OPPOSITE: (front to back) Grilled Potato Salad, Grilled and Chilled Chicken Salad with Toasted Almonds and Grapes, Grilled Chicken Spinach Salad with Sesame Soy Vinaigrette

# Grilled Chicken Spinach Salad with Sesame Soy Vinaigrette

This recipe has popped up in various incarnations over the last twenty years in the Purple Parrot Café. This is great for a spring lunch for visiting guests. The dressing holds refrigerated for two weeks. The chicken can be grilled a day or two ahead of time and held in the refrigerator. Grilled shrimp or pork can be substituted for the chicken.

Six 5–6 oz boneless, skinless chicken breasts

¼ cup No-stick Grilling Marinade for Poultry (page 206)

1 tsp Poultry Seasoning (page 213)

2 lbs fresh spinach, cleaned, stems removed

1 cup shredded carrots

¾ cup shredded red cabbage

1 cup very thinly sliced celery, on bias

1 small cantaloupe, peeled and cut into 1-inch cubes

1 recipe Sesame Soy Vinaigrette (recipe follows)

Brush the chicken breasts with the marinade and refrigerate for 1 hour.

Sprinkle the chicken with the Poultry Seasoning.

Prepare the grill. Cook the chicken over direct high heat for 10–12 minutes, turning once during the grilling process.

Remove the chicken from the grill and allow to cool completely.

Place the cleaned spinach, carrots, cabbage, celery, and cantaloupe in a large mixing bowl. Stir the vinaigrette well and pour it over the salad. Toss well and divide onto serving dishes. Slice each chicken breast into 5–6 thin strips and arrange them on the salad. Serve immediately.

YIELD: **6 servings**

(continued)

# Sesame Soy Vinaigrette

1 Tbl dry mustard

½ cup sugar

⅓ cup soy sauce

½ cup rice wine vinegar

2 Tbl white vinegar

1 Tbl sesame seed oil

2 cups canola or vegetable oil

Mix together the mustard, sugar, soy sauce, and vinegars. Slowly add the oils using a wire whisk. Refrigerate for 2 hours and stir well before serving.

YIELD: 3½ cups

*"This is great for a spring lunch for visiting guests. . . . Grilled shrimp or pork can be substituted for the chicken."*

# Grilled and Chilled Chicken Salad with Toasted Almonds and Grapes

Chicken salad is a Southern staple. My grandmother made the best. On special occasions she always added either grapes or almonds. In her honor, I have added both.

2 lbs boneless, skinless chicken breasts

½ cup No-stick Grilling Marinade for Poultry (page 206)

2 tsp Poultry Seasoning (page 213)

½ cup mayonnaise

⅓ cup sour cream

1 Tbl honey

1 Tbl Dijon mustard

1 tsp Lawry's Seasoned Salt

2 Tbl freshly squeezed orange juice

¼ tsp freshly ground black pepper

½ cup slivered almonds, toasted

½ cup minced celery

¼ cup minced green onions

½ lb red seedless grapes, halved

1 Tbl chopped parsley

Brush the chicken breasts with the no-stick marinade and refrigerate 1 hour. Sprinkle the chicken with the Poultry Seasoning.

Prepare the grill. Cook chicken over direct medium heat for 10–14 minutes, turning once during the grilling process.

Remove the chicken from the grill and allow to cool completely.

While the chicken is cooling, combine the mayonnaise, sour cream, honey, mustard, seasoning salt, orange juice, and black pepper in a mixing bowl. Dice the cooled chicken into bite-sized pieces. Fold the chicken, almonds, celery, green onions, and grapes into the mayonnaise mixture. Garnish with fresh chopped parsley.

YIELD: 6 servings

# Grilled Tenderloin Salad

A good use for leftover whole grilled beef tenderloin. Substitute cabbages such as Savoy, bok choy, or your mama's green cabbage.

½ cup soy sauce

2 tsp freshly ground black pepper

⅓ cup brown sugar

1 Tbl minced fresh garlic

1 cup rice vinegar

2 Tbl peeled and minced fresh ginger

1 tsp lime zest

5 Tbl fresh lime juice

1 Tbl minced fresh jalapeño

1 tsp crushed red pepper

2 pounds beef tenderloin

¼ cup very thinly sliced shallots

1 seedless cucumber, cut in half lengthwise, seeds removed, and sliced thin

4 green onions, cut into ½-inch-long pieces

1 tsp kosher salt

1 cup cilantro leaves, washed and dried

6 cups shredded napa cabbage

1 cup shredded red cabbage

2 cups shredded romaine lettuce

1½ cups fresh bean sprouts

¼ cup toasted sesame seeds

Combine the soy sauce, black pepper, brown sugar, garlic, vinegar, ginger, lime zest and juice, jalapeño, and crushed red pepper in a mixing bowl.

Rub approximately ⅓ cup of the soy-lime mixture over the surface of the beef tenderloin. Wrap the tenderloin in plastic and allow it to marinate for 30 minutes.

Prepare the grill. Sear the tenderloin over direct medium heat for 10–15 minutes. Move to indirect medium heat and cook to medium rare (135 degrees), 20–25 minutes.

Remove meat from the grill and allow to rest for 20 minutes.

Combine all of the vegetables, salt, and cilantro in a mixing bowl and toss with the remaining dressing. Divide the salad onto serving dishes.

Slice the beef into ¼-inch-thick slices and arrange the slices on the salad. Sprinkle with the toasted sesame seeds and serve immediately.

YIELD: 6 servings

# Grilled Ruby Red Shrimp Salad

Ruby reds are a deep-water shrimp that have a flavor almost akin to Florida lobster. If you have trouble finding them, feel free to substitute any variety of wild American shrimp.

2½ lbs ruby red shrimp, peeled and deveined

¼ cup No-stick Grilling Marinade for Shrimp (page 209)

1 tsp kosher salt

½ tsp Old Bay seasoning

⅛ tsp freshly ground black pepper

1 cup mayonnaise

2 hard-boiled eggs, chopped

1 Tbl capers, rinsed and chopped fine

½ tsp Lawry's Seasoned Salt

1 Tbl Dijon mustard

1 Tbl sweet pickle relish

½ cup minced celery

2 Tbl minced red onions

1 tsp lemon juice

⅛ tsp freshly ground black pepper

1 Tbl chopped parsley

1 Tbl chopped chives

Using a pastry brush, coat the shrimp with the no-stick marinade. Allow shrimp to marinate for 30 minutes. Sprinkle the shrimp with the salt, Old Bay seasoning, and pepper.

Place the grill screen over direct high heat and allow it to preheat. Place shrimp on the hot grill screen and cook 6–8 minutes, turning once. Remove the shrimp and allow to cool down completely.

In a mixing bowl, combine the remaining ingredients except for the chives. Roughly chop the chilled shrimp and fold into the mayonnaise mixture.

Cover and store refrigerated until ready to serve. Garnish with the chopped chives before serving.

YIELD: **6 servings**

# Smoked Tuna Pasta Salad

The tuna can be smoked a few days in advance. While you've got the smoker fired up, smoke an extra pound of tuna until medium well, remove from the grill, chop it fine, add 1 teaspoon Creole Seasoning (page 212), 1 teaspoon freshly ground black pepper, and 1 cup Hellmann's mayonnaise for a great smoked tuna dip.

1 lb fresh tuna (whole loin or fresh steaks)

2½ cups Creamy Balsamic Vinaigrette Dressing (page 74)

1–2 cups wood chips, soaked in water

½ lb dry rotini (or spiral) pasta

1 cup sliced black olives

1 cup peeled and small dice red onions

½ cup small dice red bell peppers

½ cup small dice green bell peppers

1 cup medium dice fresh tomatoes

1 tsp salt

1 tsp freshly ground black pepper

¼ cup chopped fresh parsley

Rub the outside of the tuna thoroughly with ½ cup of the Creamy Balsamic Vinaigrette Dressing and allow to marinate 2–3 hours.

Prepare the grill. Place wood chips over the coals to create a heavy smoke. Cook tuna over direct medium heat until tuna reaches medium–medium well, 8–10 minutes. Remove tuna and allow to cool completely. Once cooled, dice into 1-inch cubes.

Following the directions on the package of rotini, cook the pasta. Once cooked, drain well and rinse thoroughly with cool water. Drain completely.

Place the pasta in a large mixing bowl. Add all of the remaining ingredients and the tuna and mix well.

Chill for 2–3 hours before serving.

YIELD: 6 servings

(continued)

# Creamy Balsamic Vinaigrette Dressing

3 egg yolks

2 eggs

½ tsp dry mustard

2 Tbl minced garlic

½ tsp white pepper

1 tsp garlic salt

⅛ tsp cayenne pepper

2 Tbl chopped parsley

2 tsp dried oregano

2 Tbl red wine vinegar

¼ cup balsamic vinegar

1 cup prepared ranch dressing

1 cup cottonseed oil or
vegetable oil

1 tsp salt

Combine all ingredients in the bowl of a food processor except ranch dressing and oil. Mix well. With the machine running, slowly drizzle in ranch dressing and then cottonseed oil. Refrigerate until ready to use. This dressing will hold 1 week refrigerated.

YIELD: 3 cups

# Garden to the Grill

# Grilled Corn

If it's not summer, and fresh corn isn't in season, don't bother with this recipe. If the corn's coming in, make it daily.

6 ears fresh corn

½ cup unsalted butter, softened

1¼ tsp kosher salt

1 tsp freshly ground black pepper

¾ tsp Poultry Seasoning (page 213)

Peel back the husks of the corn, but do not remove. Remove all of the corn silk. Using a pastry brush, coat the corn kernels with the softened butter.

Combine the salt, pepper, and Poultry Seasoning and sprinkle it evenly on the corn. Replace the husks in their natural position. Tear six 3 × 6-inch pieces of aluminum foil and wrap one piece around each ear of corn.

Prepare the grill. Cook the corn on direct medium heat for 20 minutes, turning every 5 minutes. Remove from the grill. Remove the husks and serve immediately, or hold in a 180-degree oven until needed.

YIELD: 6 servings

*"If the corn's coming in, make it daily."*

# Grilled Vidalia Onions

If Vidalias are not available, Texas 10/20s will work just fine. A true Bermuda onion will do, too. The No-stick Grilling Marinade for Beef (page 205) also works with this recipe.

12 wooden or metal skewers, soaked in water for 45 minutes

2 Vidalia onions (approximately 1 lb), cut into ½-inch-thick circles

2 Tbl No-stick Grilling Marinade for Vegetables (page 210)

2 tsp freshly ground black pepper

Run 2 soaked skewers through the side of each onion, so that each onion slice looks like a double-handled lollipop. Wrap the skewers in foil.

Brush the no-stick marinade on the onions and allow them to marinate for 15 minutes.

Sprinkle the onions with the black pepper.

Prepare the grill. Cook onions over direct medium heat for 3 minutes. Rotate the onions one quarter turn, cooking for 2 minutes more. Turn the onions over and cook for 3 minutes covered. Remove onions from the grill and remove aluminum foil. Serve immediately.

YIELD: **6–8 servings**

# Stuffed Tomatoes

These must be cooked along the outer edge of the grill. Homemade bread crumbs always taste better than store-bought.

6 large tomatoes, not too ripe

2 Tbl olive oil

¼ cup minced shallots

2 Tbl minced yellow onions

¼ tsp salt

¼ tsp freshly ground black pepper

½ cup tomato pulp, scooped from tomatoes and chopped

1 Tbl fresh orange juice

1 tsp Worcestershire sauce

¼ cup Pesto (page 21)

⅓ cup Italian seasoned bread crumbs

Remove the core of the tomatoes and slice across the very top of each tomato.

Using a teaspoon, scoop out about 1 tablespoon of the pulp from each tomato and roughly chop it.

Over low heat, heat olive oil in a small sauté pan. In the sauté pan, cook the shallots, onions, salt, and black pepper for 5 minutes. Add the tomato pulp, orange juice, and Worcestershire sauce, and cook 4–5 minutes more. Remove from the heat and stir in the Pesto.

Divide the mixture evenly among the hollowed-out tomatoes. Sprinkle bread crumbs over tops of the stuffed tomatoes.

Prepare the grill. Cook tomatoes over direct medium heat for 5 minutes, rotating tomatoes one quarter turn and cooking for 3–5 minutes more. Serve immediately.

**YIELD: 6 servings**

# Grilled Sweet Potatoes

Be careful—due to the naturally occurring sugars, sweet potatoes burn easily.
These taste great.

4 sweet potatoes
   (approximately 2 lbs)
½ cup unsalted butter, softened
2 Tbl brown sugar
¼ tsp cinnamon
1 tsp hot sauce
½ tsp kosher salt
¼ tsp freshly ground black
   pepper

Peel sweet potatoes and cut into ½-inch-thick slices.

In a small mixing bowl, blend together butter, brown sugar, cinnamon, and hot sauce.

Place sweet potatoes on a baking sheet and lightly brush the surfaces with the butter mixture.

Prepare the grill. Place sweet potatoes over direct medium heat, buttered side down. Brush the tops with the butter mixture and cook the potatoes for 12–15 minutes, turning once. When the potatoes are fork tender, remove them from the grill. Brush with any remaining butter and sprinkle with the salt and pepper.

YIELD: 6 servings

# Grilled Yellow Squash and Zucchini

This can be done with all squash or all zucchini. This is my favorite way to eat these vegetables. Place them in the refrigerator after grilling and serve as a cold canapé.

2 large yellow squash, cut on the bias into ½-inch pieces

2 large zucchini, cut on the bias into ½-inch pieces

1 Tbl kosher salt

½ cup No-stick Grilling Marinade for Vegetables (page 210)

1 tsp freshly ground black pepper

Place the squash and the zucchini on a paper-towel-lined baking sheet and sprinkle salt over all. Let squash sit 20 minutes.

Pat the surfaces of the squash dry. Use a pastry brush to coat both sides of the squash with the no-stick marinade.

Prepare the grill. Cook over direct high heat for 6–8 minutes, turning once. Remove from grill and immediately sprinkle with the black pepper.

Serve hot or cold.

YIELD: 6 servings

# Shrimp-Stuffed Portobello Mushrooms

Not the easiest recipe in the book, but certainly worth the effort. The portobellos must be fresh and firm. Floppy mushrooms need not apply.

2 Tbl olive oil

1 lb shrimp, small

2 tsp Old Bay seasoning

8 ounces cream cheese, softened

¼ cup unsalted butter, softened

1 egg, slightly beaten

½ tsp kosher salt

1 tsp freshly ground black pepper

½ tsp dry thyme

¼ tsp dry oregano

½ tsp chopped fresh rosemary

1 Tbl chopped fresh chives

1 Tbl chopped fresh basil

2 tsp chopped fresh dill

2 tsp sherry vinegar

½ tsp Worcestershire sauce

½ cup coarse unseasoned bread crumbs

¼ cup sour cream

6–8 whole portobello mushrooms, stems removed, gills removed

½ cup No-stick Grilling Marinade for Vegetables (page 210)

Heat the olive oil in a large sauté pan over high heat. Season shrimp with the Old Bay seasoning and cook 6–7 minutes, until shrimp is just done. Remove shrimp from the heat and allow to cool completely. Roughly chop the shrimp.

While the shrimp is cooling, beat the cream cheese and butter with the paddle attachment of an electric mixer. Beat for several minutes, until the mixture becomes light and airy. Add the beaten egg, salt, pepper, herbs, vinegar, Worcestershire sauce, bread crumbs, and sour cream. Mix well. Fold the shrimp into the cream cheese mixture.

Coat the bottoms of the portobellos with the no-stick marinade. Divide the shrimp mixture evenly into the mushrooms.

Prepare the grill. Cook mushrooms over direct medium heat for 12–15 minutes, rotating twice. Serve immediately.

YIELD: 6–8 servings

# Grilled Eggplant

For a nice variation, use Japanese eggplant, cut lengthwise.

1 large eggplant, cut into
½-inch-thick round slices

1 Tbl kosher salt

¼ cup No-stick Grilling
Marinade for Vegetables
(page 210)

2 tsp freshly ground black
pepper

Sprinkle the eggplant with the salt and place on paper towels. Allow the eggplant to sit for 30 minutes.

Using paper towels, pat the eggplant wheels dry and brush them with the marinade. Allow to sit for 10 minutes.

Prepare the grill. Cook the eggplant over direct high heat for 2 minutes and rotate one quarter turn. Cook 2 more minutes, then turn each slice over and cook for 3 more minutes. Remove from the grill and sprinkle the eggplant with the freshly ground black pepper. Serve hot or cold.

YIELD: **4–6 servings**

OPPOSITE: (front to back) Grilled Radicchio, Grilled Sweet Potatoes, Grilled Eggplant, Skewered Marinated Onions, Stufffed Tomatoes

# Grilled Radicchio

Belgian endive and other petite lettuces work well, too.

2 heads radicchio, cut into
    4 wedges each

¼ cup No-stick Grilling
    Marinade for Vegetables
    (page 210)

2 tsp kosher salt

1 tsp freshly ground black
    pepper

¼ cup olive oil

1 Tbl balsamic vinegar

2 Tbl orange juice

1 tsp Creole mustard

1 tsp minced shallots

1 tsp chopped fresh thyme

Place a toothpick through the center of each radicchio wedge to prevent the leaves from falling off. Brush radicchio with the marinade and sprinkle with salt and pepper. Prepare the grill. Cook radicchio directly over medium heat for 5–6 minutes, turning once.

Meanwhile, whisk together the olive oil, vinegar, orange juice, mustard, shallots, and fresh thyme.

Remove the radicchio from the grill and drizzle the olive oil mixture over the radicchio. Serve immediately.

YIELD: **6–8 servings**

# Grilled Asparagus Skewers

Be careful when skewering the asparagus. Small stalks won't work with this recipe.
Buy the largest asparagus that you can find.

30 asparagus spears

12 wooden skewers, soaked in water overnight

½ cup No-stick Grilling Marinade for Vegetables (page 210)

1 Tbl kosher salt

1 tsp freshly ground black pepper

Trim the tough ends from the asparagus. Line 5 asparagus spears next to one another similar to fingers on a hand. Using 2 skewers, skewer them crosswise with 1 skewer just below the tips and the other about 1 inch from the bottom. Take your time, being careful not to split the asparagus.

Brush the asparagus with the marinade and sprinkle them with the salt and pepper.

Grill the asparagus on direct medium heat for 6–8 minutes, turning once after 4 minutes.

Remove from the grill and serve.

YIELD: 6 servings

# Caramelized Onions

These are one of the most used components in my larder. They can be made in a skillet indoors and cooked over low to medium heat for 20–30 minutes, stirring often. Be careful not to burn.

1 quart peeled and sliced
    yellow onions, cut into
    ¼-inch-thick slices

1 Tbl kosher salt

¼ cup hot clarified butter

1 tsp freshly ground black
    pepper

Sprinkle the onions with the salt and place them in a colander for 30 minutes.

Pat the onions dry with paper towels.

Toss onions with the hot clarified butter.

Tear an 18- × 18-inch sheet of aluminum foil. Spread the onions out on one half of the foil. Sprinkle the onions with black pepper. Fold the foil over the onions and fold all edges to create a sealed package.

Prepare the grill. Place the package on direct medium heat and cook 30–40 minutes. Shake and turn the package every 7–8 minutes.

YIELD: 2½ cups

OPPOSITE: Grilled Asparagus Skewers, Caramelized Onions, Marinated and Grilled Mushrooms

# Marinated and Grilled Mushrooms

Don't be alarmed by the amount of mushrooms at the beginning of the cooking process; they cook down quickly, and you'll wish you'd cooked more.

1 lb button mushrooms

1 lb shiitake mushrooms

3 large portobello mushrooms

½ cup No-stick Grilling Marinade for Vegetables (page 210)

1 tsp kosher salt

1 tsp freshly ground black pepper

Trim the stems on the button mushrooms so that they are even with the bottom of the mushroom. Gently remove and discard the stems of the shiitake mushrooms. Remove and discard the stems from the portobello mushrooms. Using a small spoon, scrape the underside of the portobello mushrooms to remove the dark gills. Cut the portobello mushrooms into 6–8 wedges.

Place the mushrooms in a large mixing bowl with the no-stick marinade. Use a rubber spatula (or your hands) to mix and coat all of the mushrooms with the no-stick marinade. Marinate for 30 minutes. Sprinkle the marinated mushrooms with the salt and pepper.

Prepare the grill. Preheat a grill screen over medium direct heat. Spread the marinated mushrooms on the hot grill screen and cook 10–14 minutes, turning once while cooking.

As soon as the hot mushrooms come off of the grill, place them in the no-stick marinade and toss evenly to coat all of the mushrooms. Keep the mushrooms in a warm place for at least 15 minutes before serving. Best when allowed to marinate in the refrigerator overnight.

Serve warm or chilled.

YIELD: **6 servings**

# Tobacco Onions

One of the most underrated condiment/side items out there. The onions get their name from their appearance after being fried. The raw onion must be sliced as thin as possible. A mandoline or meat slicer works best. Tobacco Onions must be fried at the last minute.

1–2 large red onions, shaved crosswise into paper-thin circles (about 2½ cups)

¼ cup white vinegar

1 Tbl kosher salt

¼ tsp freshly ground black pepper

2–3 quarts vegetable oil for frying

1 cup milk

2 eggs

3 cups seasoned flour

Combine the onions, vinegar, salt, and pepper in a medium-sized mixing bowl and let sit for 30 minutes.

Heat oil to 350 degrees in an 8-quart heavy-duty sauce pot or a large cast-iron skillet.

Whisk together the milk and eggs in a mixing bowl. Place onions in the milk mixture, then drain well.

Place the seasoned flour in another mixing bowl, and toss onions in the flour, making sure they are coated well. Remove onions from the bowl and shake off any excess flour.

Place half of the coated onions in the hot oil. Using a slotted spoon, gently turn 2–3 times. Fry 3–4 minutes. Remove onions and place on paper towel–lined baking sheet to drain.

Fry the remaining onions and serve immediately.

YIELD: 6–8 servings

*"The onions get their name from their appearance after being fried."*

# Jalapeño Chips

Frying jalapeños takes a little of the heat out. These are good when used like croutons in a tossed salad, or on nachos, or just straight out of the fryer.

3–4 quarts peanut oil for frying

1 cup all-purpose flour

2 Tbl Creole Seasoning (page 212)

1 Tbl, plus 1 tsp salt

2 cups buttermilk

1 egg

1½ cups cornmeal

½ cup corn flour

2 cups sliced canned jalapeños

Heat oil to 350 degrees in a cast-iron skillet.

Mix the flour, 1 tablespoon Creole Seasoning, and 1 teaspoon salt in a bowl. Beat together the buttermilk and egg in a second bowl. In a third bowl, combine cornmeal, corn flour, and remaining seasoning.

Place the jalapeños in the seasoned flour first, knock off excess flour, and place in buttermilk mixture. Drain well. Coat with cornmeal mixture and drop into fryer. Fry until golden, 5–7 minutes.

YIELD: 3–4 cups

OPPOSITE: Caramelized Onions, Tobacco Onions, Jalapeño Chips

*"Grouper is my favorite of all of the Gulf fish. It is firm, and grills better than any other."*

Gulf to the Grill

# Grouper with Black Bean, Corn, and Tomato Salsa

Grouper is my favorite of all of the Gulf fish. It is firm, and grills better than any other. If you don't have grouper, red snapper is a good substitute. The black bean and corn salsa can be served alone, as a dip, before dinner, or as a side dish with grilled chicken.

6 grouper filets, 6–8 oz each

½ cup No-stick Grilling Marinade for Seafood (page 208)

1 Tbl kosher salt

¼ tsp freshly ground black pepper

Black Bean, Corn, and Tomato Salsa (recipe follows)

Rub the fish filets with the marinade and refrigerate for 20 minutes. Season the fish with the salt and black pepper.

Prepare the grill. Place the fish on direct high heat and cook until opaque in the center, 8–10 minutes. Turn the fish once while cooking. Do not overcook.

Serve with the salsa.

YIELD: 6 servings

(continued)

# Black Bean, Corn, and Tomato Salsa

1 Tbl olive oil

¼ cup minced yellow onions

2 tsp minced garlic

½ tsp salt

½ tsp cumin

¼ tsp coriander

⅛ tsp dry oregano

1 can Rotel tomatoes (10 oz)

1 cup canned black beans,
  drained and rinsed

1 cup fresh sweet corn, cut
  from the cob

¼ cup thinly sliced green
  onions

2 tsp fresh lime juice

Place the olive oil in a small stainless-steel sauce pot over medium heat. Add the onions, garlic, salt, cumin, coriander, and oregano to the warm oil and cook 5 minutes, stirring often. Do not brown. Add the Rotel tomatoes and simmer for 2–3 minutes. Add the black beans and corn, and cook 5 minutes more. Stir in the thinly sliced green onions and lime juice, and remove from the heat.

Best if made at least 1 day in advance. Allow salsa to reach room temperature before serving.

YIELD: 3 cups

# Marinated Cedar-Plank Salmon

You can purchase smaller cedar planks and grill the salmon individually to be served on individual plates.

2 Tbl freshly squeezed lemon juice

⅓ cup No-stick Marinade for Seafood (page 208)

6 salmon filets, 7–8 oz each

2 tsp kosher salt

1 tsp freshly ground black pepper

1 large cedar plank, soaked for 1 hour in water

⅓ cup olive oil

1 Tbl Dijon mustard

1 Tbl balsamic vinegar

2 tsp garlic powder

2 tsp minced shallots

Combine the lemon juice with the no-stick marinade. Brush the salmon filets with the mixture, and sprinkle with the salt and black pepper.

Blot the soaked cedar plank dry. Combine the olive oil, mustard, vinegar, garlic powder, and shallot in a mixing bowl. Brush this mixture on the cedar plank.

Prepare the grill. Place the cedar plank, marinated side up, over direct high heat until it begins to smoke.

Arrange the salmon filets on the plank, leaving space between each one, and move the plank to indirect high heat. Cook until the salmon is just pink in the center, 10–12 minutes.

YIELD: 6 servings

# Pompano in a Foil Bag

Make sure that the foil is sealed well when cooking. Don't open the foil packages until they are sitting in front of your guests. Better still, allow your guests to open their own package. The wonderful aroma that rises when the foil is opened is something each person should personally experience. Be careful when handling the hot foil.

8 Tbl unsalted butter

¼ cup small dice yellow onions

¾ cup small julienne carrots

½ cup thinly sliced celery

1 cup small dice leeks

2 tsp minced garlic

½ tsp salt

2½ tsp Creole Seasoning (page 212)

⅛ tsp Old Bay seasoning

½ cup white wine

2 Tbl fresh lemon juice

2 tsp chopped fresh thyme

Six 12 × 18 pieces of aluminum foil

2 Tbl olive oil

6 pompano filets (7–8 oz)

In a medium sauté pan, melt the first 2 tablespoons of butter over medium heat. Place the onions and carrots in the melted butter and cook for 3–4 minutes. Add in the celery, leeks, garlic, salt, ½ teaspoon Creole Seasoning, and Old Bay seasoning, and cook for 5 minutes. Add the wine, lemon juice, and fresh thyme, and allow the mixture to reduce until a thick glaze is formed. Remove from heat.

Lay the foil sheets out on a flat surface. Brush the center of each sheet with olive oil. Place the pompano filets on the oiled foil and season them with the remaining 2 teaspoons Creole Seasoning. Divide the cooked vegetable mixture between the pompano filets and spread evenly to cover the top of the fish. Top each fish with 1 tablespoon of cold butter.

Fold the foil over the fish and crimp the edges of the foil tightly.

Prepare the grill. Cook the foil packages over direct medium heat for 12–14 minutes. Remove from the grill and serve.

YIELD: 6 servings

# Redfish on the Half Shell with Lemon Garlic Beurre Blanc

This is the true fish-eater's way to eat fresh fish. Don't be alarmed by the smell of the scales when you first put them on the grill. The odor goes away quickly, and it doesn't affect the flavor of the fish. Cooking fish with the skin on keeps the fish moist. The skin will char, but don't worry, you'll be serving it skin side down and the fork-tender fish will lift right up.

Six 9–11 oz redfish filets, skin on, scales on

¼ cup No-stick Grilling Marinade for Seafood (page 208)

2 tsp Creole Seasoning (page 212)

1 recipe Lemon Garlic Beurre Blanc (page 217)

Brush the flesh side of the filets with the no-stick marinade and season with Creole Seasoning.

Prepare the grill. Place the fish, flesh side down, over direct high heat. Cook 3 minutes and then turn the fish over. Continue cooking until the fish becomes opaque in the center, 9–10 more minutes, turning once.

Remove the fish from the grill and serve, skin side down. Top with the Lemon Garlic Beurre Blanc.

YIELD: 6 servings

# Grilled Crab Cakes with Roasted Tomato Tartar Sauce

A very tricky recipe to pull off, but worth the effort. A grill screen is a must. These crab cakes can also be sautéed in a skillet with a light oil or clarified butter.

2 Tbl chopped parsley

1 tsp hot sauce

1 tsp kosher salt

1 egg

2 egg yolks

1 cup mayonnaise

1 cup sour cream

1 tsp Creole Seasoning (page 212)

2 tsp lemon zest

1 tsp Old Bay seasoning

1 lb all lump crabmeat

2 cups coarse plain bread crumbs (Japanese panko)

olive oil to brush the grill screen

Roasted Tomato Tartar Sauce (page 222)

Mix together all ingredients except crabmeat, bread crumbs, olive oil, and Roasted Tomato Tartar Sauce. Gently fold the crabmeat and ½ cup of the bread crumbs into the mayonnaise mixture.

Place the remaining bread crumbs in a shallow baking dish. Form the crab mixture into 2–3-ounce patties. Gently drop the patties into the bread crumbs. The mixture will be loose and slightly difficult to work with, so be patient. Coat the outside of the crab cakes with the bread crumbs.

Prepare the grill. Place the grill screen over direct medium heat. Once the grill screen is hot, brush it with olive oil. Arrange the crab cakes on the screen, allowing enough room to easily turn them over with a metal spatula.

Cook the crab cakes for 12–15 minutes, turning once. Remove from the grill and place them on a baking sheet. Hold the crab cakes in a warm oven if necessary while cooking any remaining crab cakes.

Serve with Roasted Tomato Tartar Sauce.

YIELD: 6–8 servings

# Cold-Smoked Tuna Steaks with Smoked Vegetables

This is a variation of a dish taught to me by my first restaurant partner and mentor, chef Nick Apostle. He served it for years in his Jackson, Mississippi, restaurant. When prepared properly, the tuna has a steaklike flavor.

Six 6–8-oz tuna steaks

1 cup Creamy Balsamic Vinaigrette Dressing (page 74)

1½ cups julienned red bell peppers

1½ cups julienned green bell peppers

1½ cups julienned red onions

1 Tbl kosher salt

2 tsp freshly ground black pepper

1–2 cups soaked wood chips

Place tuna steaks in a large Ziploc bag, and add half of the Creamy Balsamic Vinaigrette Dressing. Place the other half of the dressing in another bag with the peppers and onions. Seal both bags and refrigerate for 2 hours.

Remove the vegetables and tuna from the bags and season with the salt and pepper.

Prepare the grill or smoker for very low-heat smoking. Place the tuna steaks on the grill as far away from the heat source as possible. Place the vegetables into a metal colander and place it in the smoker with the tuna. Add wood chips to the coals and smoke the tuna and vegetables for 1½ hours, being careful to make sure the tuna does not cook (tuna should still be rare when removed from the smoker). Add more wood chips as needed to keep a heavy smoke going.

Remove tuna and vegetables from the grill. Transfer vegetables to an airtight container. Place the tuna steaks on a cookie sheet and wrap in plastic. Refrigerate both fish and vegetables for at least 3 hours. This step may be done a day in advance.

To eat: Prepare the grill. Place a grill screen over direct high heat. Spread the vegetables over the hot grill topper and cook 6–8 minutes, turning once while cooking. Remove the vegetables and the grill screen. Hold the vegetables in a warm place

until needed. Place the tuna steaks on direct high heat and cook to desired doneness, 5 minutes for medium rare. Turn the tuna once while cooking.

To serve, place a small mound of the vegetables on a serving plate. Rest the tuna steaks on top of the vegetables and serve.

YIELD: **6 servings**

# Ginger Soy Salmon

In my opinion, ginger and soy are the best complements to salmon. You can also serve the salmon on Tobacco Onions (page 91) for additional flavor and texture.

⅓ cup No-stick Grilling Marinade for Seafood (page 208)

¼ cup soy sauce

1 Tbl minced ginger

6 salmon filets (6–8 oz each)

1 recipe Ginger Soy Sauce (page 221)

Combine the seafood marinade with the soy sauce and ginger. Use a pastry brush to coat the filets. Allow the filets to marinate at room temperature for 45 minutes.

Prepare the grill. Cook the fish on direct high heat until it is just pink in the center, 7–9 minutes. Turn the fish once while cooking. Do not overcook.

Remove the fish from the grill, top with the Ginger Soy Sauce, and serve.

YIELD: 6 servings

# Grilled Cioppino

Great for a cold night or outside by the pool in summer; the more seafood the better. The ingredients list is long, but don't be intimidated. The stock can be made a few days in advance and freezes well. Feel free to substitute or delete seafood.

1½ lbs shrimp, 21–25 count, peeled, deveined, and skewered

1 lb sea scallops, skewered

1 lb redfish pieces

½ cup No-stick Grilling Marinade for Seafood (page 208)

2 Tbl olive oil

1 Tbl minced garlic

½ cup white wine

1½ quarts Cioppino Stock (recipe follows)

1 lb fresh mussels, cleaned and beards removed

1 lb jumbo lump crabmeat

Freshly chopped parsley for garnish

Toasted French bread

Rub the surface of the shrimp, scallops, and redfish with the no-stick seafood marinade and refrigerate for 20–30 minutes.

Prepare the grill. Cook the seafood over direct high heat for 6–8 minutes, turning once while cooking. Remove the seafood from the grill, and cool slightly.

Heat the olive oil in a large sauce pot over low medium heat. Add the garlic, and cook for 1 minute. Add the wine to the pot, and reduce by half. Next, add the Cioppino Stock to the pot, and bring it to a simmer. Remove the shrimp and scallops from the skewers, and cut the grilled fish into ½-inch cubes. Add the mussels to the stock and cook until they pop open, 6–7 minutes. Once the stock is simmering, add the grilled seafood and jumbo lump crabmeat. Divide the cioppino into serving dishes, and garnish with parsley. Serve with toasted French bread.

YIELD: 6–10 servings

(continued)

# Cioppino Stock

1½ cups medium dice onions

¼ cup olive oil

¼ cup butter

1½ cups finely chopped leeks, white parts only

1½ cups medium dice green bell peppers

1⅓ cups small dice carrots

1 cup medium dice celery

¼ cup finely chopped fresh fennel

2½ quarts canned chopped tomatoes, highest quality, drained, liquid reserved (approximately four 28-oz cans)

One 6-oz can tomato paste

2½ quarts water or stock

2 Tbl salt

1½ Tbl Tabasco sauce

1 Tbl dried oregano

1 Tbl dried basil

1 Tbl dried thyme

3 bay leaves

1 Tbl Creole Seasoning (page 212)

Sauté onions in olive oil and butter. Do not brown. Add leeks, green pepper, carrots, celery, and fennel and cook 5–10 minutes, until soft. Add remaining ingredients and bring to a boil. When stock begins boiling, reduce heat immediately. Cover and simmer 2 hours, stirring frequently. This stock should be made a day ahead of time and refrigerated. Remove bay leaves before using in Cioppino recipe.

YIELD: 1¼ gallons

*"Great for a cold night or outside by the pool in summer; the more seafood the better."*

# Smoked and Grilled Soft-Shell Crab

The crabs must be fresh and firm. Soft-shell crab should be purchased alive and kicking. A grill screen is a must.

6 fresh soft-shell crabs

⅓ cup No-stick Grilling Marinade for Seafood (page 208)

2 tsp kosher salt

1 tsp freshly ground black pepper

1 cup wood chips, soaked in water for 45 minutes

Using kitchen shears, remove the eyes and gills from the soft-shell crabs.

Brush the crabs with the marinade and marinate for 20 minutes. Sprinkle with salt and pepper.

Prepare the grill. Drain the water from the soaking wood chips and disperse half of the chips over the hot coals. Place the crab over indirect medium heat and cook for 12–14 minutes, turning once while smoking. Move the crabs to direct medium heat and add the remaining wood chips to the coals. Cook for 4–5 minutes, turning once. Gently remove the crabs from the grill, and serve with Basil Aioli (recipe follows).

YIELD: 6 servings

# Basil Aioli

2 egg yolks

1 tsp Dijon mustard

1 Tbl minced garlic

½ tsp kosher salt

2 tsp lemon juice

1 Tbl balsamic vinegar

1½ cups light olive oil

½ cup roughly chopped fresh basil leaves

1 tsp freshly ground black pepper

Place the egg yolks, mustard, garlic, and salt in a blender. Puree on medium speed for 1–2 minutes. Add the lemon juice and the vinegar and then slowly begin drizzling in the olive oil. If the mixture becomes too thick, use a small amount of warm water (1 tablespoon at a time) to thin it. Add basil and black pepper and continue pureeing until the basil is thoroughly incorporated. Store refrigerated until needed.

YIELD: 1½ cups

# Smoked and Fried Soft-Shell Crab

An extra step for the traditional soft-shell crab recipe, and well worth the effort. Seafood Rémoulade (page 227) or Avocado Mayonnaise (page 12) may be used instead of the tartar sauce. Smoking the soft-shell crabs before frying them adds another dimension to one of the Gulf's best delicacies.

6 fresh soft-shell crabs

⅓ cup No-stick Grilling Marinade for Seafood (page 208)

2 tsp kosher salt

1 tsp freshly ground black pepper

1 cup wood chips, soaked in water for 45 minutes

2–3 quarts vegetable oil for frying

1 cup milk

2 whole eggs

4 cups seasoned flour

Roasted Tomato Tartar Sauce (page 222)

Using kitchen shears, remove the eyes and gills from the soft-shell crabs.

Brush the crabs with the no-stick marinade and marinate for 20 minutes. Sprinkle with the salt and pepper.

Prepare the smoker. Drain the water from the wood chips and spread half of the chips over the hot coals. Place the crabs over indirect low heat. Smoke for 15 minutes, adding more chips when necessary to keep smoke billowing. Remove the crabs gently and chill.

Heat the oil to 350 degrees in an 8-quart heavy-duty sauce pot or a large cast-iron skillet.

Whisk together the milk and eggs in a mixing bowl.

Lightly coat the crabs in the seasoned flour. Place the crabs in the milk mixture and drain well. Place the crabs back in the seasoned flour, making sure that all surfaces are floured. Gently shake off excess flour. Fry crabs for 6–7 minutes, using a slotted spoon to turn them once while cooking. Remove the crabs from the oil and drain on paper towels. Serve immediately, accompanied by the Roasted Tomato Tartar Sauce.

YIELD: 6 servings

# Key Lime Grilled Shrimp with Pecan-spiked Rice

Maybe the best shrimp recipe in the book. If you can't purchase Key limes, your average, ordinary, everyday, run-of-the-mill limes work, too. Pecan-spiked Rice is also a good side dish with grilled chicken. Use the fine-cut side of a cheese grater to remove the zest from the limes before juicing them.

36 large shrimp, peeled and deveined

¼ cup No-stick Grilling Marinade for Seafood (page 208)

2 Tbl honey

1 tsp Key lime zest

2 tsp kosher salt

½ tsp freshly ground black pepper

1 recipe Pecan-spiked Rice (recipe follows)

1 recipe Key Lime Beurre Blanc (recipe follows)

Place the shrimp in a mixing bowl and add the marinade, honey, and lime zest. Marinate for 1 hour before grilling. Place a grill screen over direct high heat. Once the grill screen is pre-heated, sprinkle the shrimp with the salt and pepper and grill for 6–8 minutes, turning once while cooking.

To serve, place Pecan-spiked Rice on serving dishes. Top the rice with 6 shrimp, and ladle Key Lime Beurre Blanc over the shrimp.

YIELD: 6 servings

(continued)

# Pecan-spiked Rice

2 Tbl unsalted butter

½ cup small dice yellow
  onions

¼ cup minced shallots

1 tsp kosher salt

1 bay leaf

1 cup white rice

2 cups chicken broth, hot

¼ tsp freshly ground black
  pepper

1 cup chopped and toasted
  pecan pieces

Melt butter over medium heat in a 1½-quart sauce pot. Add onions, shallots, salt, and bay leaf and cook 4–5 minutes, stirring often to prevent browning. Add the rice and continue to cook until the grains of rice are thoroughly heated. Stir in the chicken broth and black pepper and bring the broth to a simmer. Lower the heat and cover the rice. Cook 18–20 minutes, until all liquid is absorbed. Stir in toasted pecans. Remove and discard bay leaf before serving.

**YIELD: 6 servings**

# Key Lime Beurre Blanc

⅔ cup white wine

1 Tbl white vinegar

⅓ cup fresh Key lime juice

¼ cup finely chopped shallots

1 tsp minced garlic

¼ cup whipping cream

1 lb unsalted butter, cut into
  small cubes, then chilled

1 tsp Key lime zest

1 tsp kosher salt

1 Tbl chopped fresh chives

In a small saucepan over medium heat, reduce wine, vinegar, lime juice, shallots, and garlic. When almost all liquid has evaporated, add cream. Reduce cream by half. Reduce heat slightly and incorporate the butter, adding a few pieces at a time. Stir constantly using a wire whisk until butter is completely melted. Remove from heat. Strain the sauce and add the lime zest and salt. Hold in a warm place until needed. Stir in the fresh chopped chives just before serving.

**YIELD: 2 cups**

# Old Bay Grilled Shrimp with Creole Beurre Rouge over Dirty Rice

I love Old Bay seasoning on shrimp, and everyone who knows me knows it. Now you know, too.

36 large shrimp, peeled and deveined

½ cup No-stick Grilling Marinade for Shrimp (page 209)

2 tsp Old Bay seasoning

1 Tbl freshly ground black pepper

1 recipe Creole Beurre Rouge (page 224)

Using a pastry brush, coat the shrimp evenly with the marinade. Allow shrimp to marinate for 20 minutes. Sprinkle the shrimp with the Old Bay seasoning and black pepper.

Prepare the grill. Place a grill screen on top of the grill and pre-heat. Place the shrimp on the grate over direct high heat and cook for 6–8 minutes, turning once.

Place the cooked shrimp on a bed of Dirty Rice and top with the Creole Beurre Rouge.

**YIELD: 6 servings**

## Dirty Rice

1 Tbl bacon fat or canola oil

2 oz ground beef

2 oz ground pork

½ cup diced onions

¼ cup diced celery

¼ cup diced bell peppers

2 tsp minced garlic

1 bay leaf

1 Tbl Poultry Seasoning (page 213)

1 tsp dry mustard

1 cup rice

2 cups pork stock, hot

Heat the bacon fat in a 1-quart sauce pot over high heat. Add the ground beef and pork, and brown. Stir in the vegetables and garlic, and continue to cook 5–6 minutes. Stir in the bay leaf, Poultry Seasoning, mustard, and rice, and cook until the rice is thoroughly heated. Stir in the pork stock, and reduce heat to low. Cover the sauce pot and cook 18 minutes. Remove bay leaf before serving.

**YIELD: 3 cups**

# Grilled Shrimp over Garlic Cheese Grits

It started in North Carolina with Bill Neal and migrated to Mississippi via Oxford chef John Currence. This is my version for the outdoor grill. Never use instant grits.

36 toothpicks

4 oz andouille sausage, cut into matchstick-sized strips

36 large shrimp, peeled, butterflied, and deveined

2 Tbl olive oil

1 Tbl Creole Seasoning (page 212)

Soak the toothpicks in water for 20–30 minutes.

Place one piece of andouille sausage lengthwise down the center of each shrimp. Close each shrimp by sticking the toothpick across the open side to ensure that the andouille does not fall out. Brush the shrimp with the olive oil and sprinkle them with the Creole Seasoning.

Prepare the grill. Place a grill screen over direct high heat. Place the shrimp on the hot grill screen and cook 6–8 minutes, turning once.

Remove and serve with Garlic Cheese Grits (recipe follows).

YIELD: 6 servings

## Garlic Cheese Grits

1 Tbl bacon grease or canola oil

1 Tbl minced garlic

1 tsp salt

2 cups milk

2 cups chicken broth

1 cup grits

1 tsp Creole Seasoning (page 212)

1 tsp hot sauce

8 oz sharp cheddar cheese, shredded

4 oz cream cheese

Melt bacon grease over low heat in a 1½-quart sauce pot. Add garlic and salt, and cook for 1–2 minutes, being careful not to brown the garlic. Add milk and broth and increase heat. Bring to a simmer and slowly pour in the grits. Lower heat and cook grits for 15 minutes, stirring often.

Add remaining ingredients and stir until cheeses are melted. Serve immediately.

YIELD: 8 servings

# Grilled Soft-Shell Crab with Cucumber-Dill Dressing

The Cucumber-Dill Dressing can also be used as a salad dressing or with petite tomato sandwiches.

6 large or jumbo fresh soft-shell crabs

¼ cup olive oil

1 Tbl kosher salt

½ Tbl freshly ground black pepper

1 recipe Grilled Vidalia Onions (page 78)

1 recipe Cucumber-Dill Dressing (page 225)

Using kitchen shears, remove the eyes and gills from the soft-shell crabs. Brush the crabs with the olive oil and season with salt and pepper.

Prepare the grill. Cook the crab over direct high heat for a total of 8–10 minutes. Rotate the crabs a quarter turn after the first 3 minutes of cooking and gently flip them once while cooking.

While the crabs are cooking, prepare the grilled onions. To serve, place 1 skewered onion on a plate, set the grilled crab on the onion, and drizzle with the cucumber dressing.

YIELD: 6 servings

# Skewered Scallops over Mushroom Risotto

Don't be intimidated. Risotto is easy. Just take your time.

2½–3 lbs large sea scallops

6 long metal skewers

½ cup No-stick Grilling
Marinade for Seafood
(page 208)

2 tsp kosher salt

1 tsp freshly ground black
pepper

1 recipe Mushroom Risotto
(recipe follows)

Divide the scallops evenly onto the 6 skewers. Brush the scallops with the marinade and allow them to marinate at room temperature for 15 minutes. Sprinkle the scallops with the salt and pepper. Cook over direct high heat until the scallops are opaque in the center, 5–7 minutes. Turn the scallops once while cooking.

Place the risotto on serving dishes and remove the scallops from the skewers. Place the scallops atop Mushroom Risotto and serve.

YIELD: 6 servings

(continued)

*"Risotto is easy. Just take your time."*

# Mushroom Risotto

5 Tbl unsalted butter

3 Tbl minced shallots

2 cups Arborio rice

4–6 cups chicken stock, heated

1 Tbl kosher salt, added to the
  chicken stock

¾ lb wild mushrooms
  (shiitakes, porcinis, morels,
  chanterelles, creminis,
  portobellos, oysters),
  cleaned and sliced

1 cup heavy cream

½ cup freshly grated Parmesan
  cheese

2 Tbl chopped fresh parsley

2 tsp chopped fresh thyme

1 tsp freshly ground black
  pepper

In a very large skillet, heat 3 tablespoons of butter over medium heat and add shallots. Cook until the shallots become soft. Add rice. Stir constantly to prevent rice from browning. The grains of rice need to get hot. Add 1½ cups of hot stock and lower heat until the stock is barely simmering. Continue to stir constantly.

As the stock is absorbed, add more stock in small amounts. Continue this process until the rice has become slightly tender. In a separate skillet, place the remaining 2 tablespoons of butter over medium heat. Add mushrooms and sauté until soft. Add the mushrooms to the risotto. When rice is almost completely cooked, add cream and stir slowly until absorbed. Remove from heat and stir in cheese, fresh herbs, and pepper. Serve immediately.

YIELD: 6–8 servings

# Snapper Pontchartrain

This topping can also be served on top of filet mignon or tournedos of beef.

6 red snapper filets, 6–8 oz each

½ cup No-stick Grilling Marinade for Seafood (page 208)

1 Tbl kosher salt

¼ tsp freshly ground black pepper

1 Tbl Clarified Butter (page 218)

2½ cups sliced button mushrooms

2 tsp minced garlic

¾ cup sliced green onions

2 ounces white wine

8 ounces jumbo lump crabmeat

1 tsp hot sauce

¾ cup Lemon Meunière Sauce (page 218)

Lemon wedges, for serving

Chopped fresh parsley, for serving

Rub the fish filets with the no-stick marinade and refrigerate 20 minutes. Season the fish with the salt and black pepper.

Prepare the grill. Place the fish on direct high heat and cook until opaque in the center, 8–10 minutes. Turn the fish once while cooking.

Heat the Clarified Butter in a large skillet over medium high heat. Place mushrooms in skillet and sauté until tender. Add garlic and green onions and cook 2–3 minutes more. Add white wine, crabmeat, and hot sauce, and cook just long enough to heat the crab. Remove from heat and add the Lemon Meunière. Remove filets from grill and place on serving dishes. Evenly divide topping over fish and serve. Garnish with lemon and fresh parsley.

YIELD: 6–8 servings

# Grilled Grouper Madeira

A mainstay in the early days of the Purple Parrot Café. Add shrimp to the topping and substitute fettuccini for the grouper for a nice pasta entrée. Good Marsala can be substituted for the Madeira.

6 grouper filets, 8 oz each

½ cup No-stick Grilling Marinade for Seafood (page 208)

1 Tbl kosher salt

¼ tsp freshly ground black pepper

2 Tbl clarified butter

4 cups sliced mushrooms

1 12–oz can artichoke hearts, drained

1½ cups sliced green onions

3 Tbl minced garlic

4 ounces Madeira wine

1 cup Lemon Meunière Sauce (page 218)

Rub the fish filets with the no-stick marinade and refrigerate for 20 minutes. Season the fish with the kosher salt and black pepper.

Prepare the grill. Cook the fish over direct high heat until opaque in the center, 8–10 minutes. Turn the fish once while cooking. Do not overcook.

In a sauté pan, cook mushrooms in clarified butter until tender. Add artichoke hearts, green onions, and garlic, and continue to cook for 3–4 minutes. Deglaze with Madeira, and reduce wine by one half. Remove from heat and add Lemon Meuniere.

Top fish with the sauce and garnish with lemon and fresh parsley.

YIELD: 6 servings

# Redfish Orleans

If you're out of fish, this sauce can also be tossed with warm rotini pasta noodles.

6 redfish filets, 6–8 oz each

½ cup No-stick Grilling Marinade for Seafood (page 208)

1 Tbl kosher salt

¼ tsp freshly ground black pepper

¼ cup olive oil

¾ pound shrimp, peeled and deveined

2½ cups sliced mushrooms

2 tsp minced garlic

¾ cup sliced green onions

¾ cup Creole Cream Sauce (page 129)

¼ cup Parmesan Cream Sauce (page 129)

Chopped fresh parsley, for serving

⅓ cup grated Romano cheese

Rub the fish filets with the marinade and refrigerate for 20 minutes. Season the fish with the salt and black pepper.

Prepare the grill. Place the fish on direct high heat and cook 4–5 minutes. Turn fish and cook another 4–5 minutes or until opaque in the center.

Heat olive oil in a large sauté pan over high heat. Sauté shrimp for 2–3 minutes, until they begin to turn pink. Add mushrooms and cook until tender. Add garlic and green onions, and cook an additional 2–3 minutes. Add Crawfish Cream Sauce and Parmesan Cream Sauce, and bring to a simmer. Remove from heat; stir in cheese. Divide evenly and spoon over fish. Garnish with chopped fresh parsley and grated Romano.

YIELD: 6 servings

# Creole Cream Sauce

2 cups heavy cream

1 Tbl Creole Seasoning
   (page 212)

2 Tbl Worcestershire sauce

2 Tbl hot sauce

1 tsp paprika

Place all ingredients in a double boiler over medium high heat and reduce by half.

YIELD: 1½ cups

# Parmesan Cream Sauce

1 quart heavy cream

½ pound Parmesan cheese,
   grated

⅓ pound Romano cheese,
   grated

2 tsp white pepper

⅛ tsp nutmeg

Bring the cream to a boil. Add cheeses and stir well. Add pepper and nutmeg.

Separately, make a light blond roux using 3 tablespoons butter and 4 tablespoons flour. Add roux to the cream/cheese mixture and continue cooking until thickened.

YIELD: 1 quart

# Bayou Redfish

The quality of tomatoes makes a big difference in the outcome of this dish. Make it in summer. This topping can be used with crab cakes or added to fried eggplant wheels.

Eight 8-oz redfish filets

½ cup No-stick Grilling
    Marinade for Seafood
    (page 208)

1 Tbl kosher salt

¼ tsp freshly ground black
    pepper

18 shrimp, large, peeled, and
    deveined

1 tsp Old Bay seasoning

3 Tbl butter

2 Tbl small dice red bell
    peppers

2 Tbl small dice green bell
    peppers

¼ cup small dice red onions

1 Tbl garlic

1½ cups diced tomatoes

1 Tbl Creole Seasoning
    (page 212)

¾ cup heavy cream

¼ cup Parmesan Cream Sauce
    (page 129)

8 ounces crawfish tail meat

Rub the fish filets with the marinade and refrigerate for 20 minutes. Season the fish with the salt and black pepper.

Prepare the grill. Cook fish over direct high heat until it becomes opaque in the center, 8–10 minutes. Turn the fish once while cooking. Do not overcook.

Season the shrimp with the Old Bay seasoning. Heat the butter in a large sauté pan over high heat and sauté shrimp 2–3 minutes. Add the bell peppers and onion, and cook for 3–4 minutes more. Add the garlic and tomatoes, and continue to cook for 5 minutes more. Stir in the Creole Seasoning, cream, and Parmesan Cream Sauce, and bring to a simmer. Cook 3–4 more minutes and stir in the crawfish tails. Once the crawfish tails are hot, remove the topping from the heat.

Place fish on serving plates and divide topping evenly over filets.

YIELD: 8 servings

*"It is important to keep the lid closed to prevent the fire from flaring up and charring the skin."*

Fowl

# Zydeco Chicken

The quality of andouille will make a huge difference in the outcome of this dish. The best andouille is made in South Louisiana. The Creole Cream Sauce has multiple uses—fish, pasta, and shrimp.

Six 5–6 oz boneless, skinless chicken breasts

½ cup No-stick Grilling Marinade for Poultry (page 206)

2 tsp Poultry Seasoning (page 213)

2 Tbl olive oil

8 ounces andouille sausage, cut in half lengthwise, then sliced into ¼-inch-thick slices

2 cups sliced button mushrooms

2 tsp minced fresh garlic

2 cups Creole Cream Sauce (page 28)

¾ cup thinly sliced green onions

1 Tbl chopped fresh parsley

Using a pastry brush, coat the chicken breasts with the marinade. Refrigerate 30 minutes. Sprinkle the breasts with the Poultry Seasoning.

Prepare the grill. Cook chicken breasts over direct high heat for 10–12 minutes, turning once during the grilling process.

Heat olive oil in a large sauté pan over high heat. Place the sausage in the hot oil and cook 6–7 minutes, stirring every 2–3 minutes. Add sliced mushrooms and cook 5 minutes more. Lower the heat to medium and add the garlic. Cook for 3 minutes more. Add the Creole Cream Sauce and bring mixture to a simmer. Cook until the mixture becomes slightly thick. Stir in green onions and fresh parsley, and remove from the heat.

Place the chicken breasts on serving dishes, and top each one with ⅓–½ cup of the topping.

YIELD: 6 servings

# Whole Roasted Citrus Chicken

Possibly the second best chicken dish I have ever eaten (the first is the beer can chicken—Yardbird with Barley and Hops Enema, page 138). Use the leftover chicken for chicken salad or spinach salad.

1 quart water

1 cup sugar

⅓ cup kosher salt

2 Tbl freshly ground black pepper

2 oranges

2 lemons

2 limes

1 whole chicken, 3½–4 lbs

1 orange, cut into quarters

1 lemon, cut into quarters

1 lime, cut into quarters

½ cup small dice yellow onions

1 tsp minced fresh garlic

1 Tbl chopped fresh thyme

2–3 Tbl olive oil

2 tsp Poultry Seasoning (page 213)

Place the water, sugar, salt, and 1 tablespoon black pepper in a sauce pot and bring to a simmer to dissolve sugar and salt. Remove from heat. Using a vegetable peeler, remove only the outer skin from the first 2 oranges, lemons, and limes, being careful not to get any of the pith (white part of the peel). Add the peelings to the brine. Squeeze all of the juice from the peeled citrus and add the juice to the brine. Place the brine in the refrigerator and allow to cool completely.

Remove giblets and neck from the chicken and submerge the chicken in the brine. Cover and refrigerate overnight.

Remove chicken from the brine and, using a paper towel, dry all surfaces of the chicken, including the cavity area.

Combine the orange, lemon, and lime quarters with the diced onions, minced garlic, and fresh thyme. Stuff the citrus-onion mixture into the cavity of the chicken.

Brush the skin of the chicken with olive oil and sprinkle the skin with Poultry Seasoning and the remaining black pepper. Tie the legs together and bend the wings back to secure them.

Prepare the grill. Cook with the breast side up over indirect medium heat until the juices run clear, or until an internal temperature of 170 degrees is reached, 1¼–1½ hours.

Place the chicken on a cutting board, and allow it to rest for 10–12 minutes before carving. Serve hot.

YIELD: 4 servings

# Basin Street Chicken

Make this when tomatoes are in season, and you'll be a happy griller.

Six 5–6 oz boneless, skinless chicken breasts

½ cup No-stick Grilling Marinade for Poultry (page 206)

2 tsp Poultry Seasoning (page 213)

2 Tbl unsalted butter

3 cups sliced mushrooms

1 tsp salt

1 tsp freshly ground black pepper

Six 1-oz slices cheddar cheese

Six 1-oz slices Monterey Jack cheese

1 recipe Caramelized Onions, hot (page 88)

1½ cups medium dice fresh tomatoes

1 Tbl chopped fresh parsley

Using a pastry brush, coat the chicken breasts with the no-stick marinade. Refrigerate 30 minutes. Sprinkle the breasts with Poultry Seasoning.

Prepare the grill. Cook chicken over direct high heat for 10–12 minutes, turning once.

While the chicken is cooking: Heat butter in a medium sauté pan over high heat. Place mushrooms, salt, and pepper in the hot butter and sauté the mushrooms for 6–7 minutes, stirring them occasionally. Drain off any excess moisture.

With the chickens on the grill, top each chicken breast with 1 slice each of both cheeses. Divide the onions and mushrooms evenly and place them atop the cheese. Close the lid to the grill and cook until cheese melts.

Place chicken on serving dishes and top with the fresh tomatoes and chopped parsley.

YIELD: **6 servings**

# Yardbird with Barley and Hops Enema

A strange name, but an excellent dish. Several companies manufacture a device that holds the beer can upright. The chicken fits around it and keeps it steady on the grill. The device is not necessary when preparing this dish, but it sure helps. If you don't want to use beer, try a can of apple juice. This is easy, and so much better than grocery store roasted chicken.

1 whole chicken, about 4 lbs
½ cup No-stick Grilling Marinade for Poultry (page 206)
1 Tbl Poultry Seasoning (page 213)
½ Tbl freshly ground black pepper
One 12-oz can of beer

Remove and discard the neck and giblets and any excess pockets of fat from the chicken. Rinse and dry the chicken.

Rub the no-stick marinade over the chicken and inside the cavity. Marinate 1 hour at room temperature. Just before cooking, sprinkle the cavity and skin with the Poultry Seasoning and black pepper.

Prepare the grill. Open the can of beer and place the chicken over the beer so that the beer can sits upright and fills the cavity of the chicken. Transfer the chicken to the grill and place over indirect medium heat. Push the bird down far enough on the can so that the legs give support to keep the chicken from falling over. Cook until an internal temperature of 170 degrees is reached or the juices run clear, approximately 1½ hours.

Carefully remove the chicken from the grill. Using a hot pad, pull the beer can from the center of the chicken and discard. Allow the chicken to rest for 10 minutes before carving.

YIELD: 4–6 servings

# Grilled Chicken with Peach BBQ sauce

The sauce has a good shelf life and can be used with pork tenderloin or smoked turkey.

1 whole chicken (2½–3 lbs),
  cut into 8 pieces
1 cup No-stick Grilling
  Marinade for Poultry
  (page 206)
1 Tbl Poultry Seasoning
  (page 213)
2 tsp freshly ground black
  pepper
Peach BBQ Sauce
  (recipe follows)

Brush the skin of the chicken pieces with the no-stick marinade and marinate at room temperature 1 hour. Sprinkle the chicken with the Poultry Seasoning and black pepper.

Prepare the grill. Cook chicken leg and thigh pieces over direct medium heat. Cook 5–6 minutes. Add the breast and wing pieces to the grill, skin side down, and cook all chicken 6–7 minutes more. Turn the chicken over and cook 7–9 minutes more. It is important to keep the lid closed to prevent the fire from flaring up and charring the skin.

Brush the chicken with the Peach BBQ Sauce twice during the last 8 minutes of cooking, and serve the remaining barbeque sauce on the side.

YIELD: **4–6 servings**

# Peach BBQ Sauce

2 tsp bacon fat or canola oil

¼ cup small dice onions

2 tsp minced garlic

1 tsp minced ginger

2 tsp small dice jalapeño

1½ cups peeled, diced fresh peaches (frozen may be substituted)

2 tsp tomato paste

½ cup brown sugar

¾ cup ketchup

⅓ cup chicken stock or broth

¼ cup orange juice

2 Tbl rice wine vinegar

2 tsp soy sauce

1 tsp Worcestershire sauce

½ cinnamon stick

⅛ tsp coriander

⅛ tsp cumin

⅛ tsp chili powder

1 tsp kosher salt

¼ tsp freshly ground black pepper

¼ tsp dry thyme, or 1 tsp freshly chopped thyme

Preheat oven to 300 degrees.

In a 2-quart ovenproof sauce pot, heat the bacon fat over low heat. Cook onions 5 minutes, stirring occasionally. Add the garlic, ginger, jalapeño, and peaches. Increase the heat to medium and cook 10 minutes, stirring often. Add the tomato paste and cook for 5 minutes more. Stir in the remaining ingredients. Cover the sauce and place in the preheated oven.

Bake for 45 minutes, stirring occasionally. Remove the cover and bake for 30 minutes more.

The sauce may be made days in advance, and is best when a day or two old. Keep refrigerated.

YIELD: 2½ cups

# Dixie Chicken

Try golden pineapple and tasso ham for a sweeter, spicier version.

Six 5–6 oz boneless, skinless
    chicken breasts

½ cup No-stick Grilling
    Marinade for Poultry
    (page 206)

2 tsp Poultry Seasoning
    (page 213)

6 canned pineapple rings

¾ lb honey-cured ham,
    shaved thin

Six 1-oz slices Swiss cheese

Using a pastry brush, coat the chicken breasts with the no-stick marinade. Refrigerate 30 minutes. Sprinkle breasts with the Poultry Seasoning.

Prepare the grill. Cook the chicken over direct high heat for 10–12 minutes, turning once.

During the last few minutes of cooking, place the pineapple rings on the grill and cook 2 minutes more, turning once.

Once cooked, but while the chicken is still on the grill, top each piece with approximately 2 ounces of shaved ham and 1 slice of Swiss cheese. Place the cover back on the grill and cook until the cheese is melted and the ham is hot. Top each breast with a ring of grilled pineapple and serve.

YIELD: **6 servings**

Make
Mine
Swine

# BBQ Ribs

South Mississippi, my part of the country, has many excellent rib joints. Unlike the vinegar-based North Carolina version, our BBQ is sweet—some say it's all the pine pollen floating around in the air that makes us crave sweet stuff. Serve the ribs dry with a side of sauce. The rub works well for beef ribs, too.

3 full racks of pork spareribs,
    3–4 lbs each (3-inch/down)

2 cups white vinegar

½ cup paprika

¼ cup garlic powder

2 Tbl onion powder

1 Tbl freshly ground black
    pepper

2 Tbl kosher salt

¼ cup brown sugar

⅓ cup sugar

1 Tbl Creole Seasoning
    (page 212)

1 recipe BBQ Sauce
    (page 220)

Place the ribs in a large roasting pan or baking dish and pour the vinegar over the ribs. Using your hand, rub all of the ribs with the vinegar and allow them to marinate for 1 hour. Drain the vinegar and dry each rack completely with paper towels.

Combine the spices, sugars, and Creole Seasoning and coat the ribs completely with the mixture. Cover and refrigerate overnight.

Prepare the grill. Cook the ribs over indirect low heat for 2½–3 hours or until they begin to pull away from the tips of the bones and the entire rack bends easily when held in the middle with a pair of tongs.

Serve ribs dry with BBQ Sauce on the side.

YIELD: 6–8 servings

# Pulled Pork

Best when served immediately out of the smoker. Good for sandwiches, or just served on a plate covered with BBQ sauce.

1 pork shoulder, 7–8 lbs

1 cup balsamic vinegar

½ cup paprika

¼ cup garlic powder

2 Tbl onion powder

1 Tbl freshly ground black pepper

2 Tbl kosher salt

¼ cup brown sugar

⅓ cup sugar

1 Tbl Creole Seasoning (page 212)

4–5 cups wood chips

1 recipe BBQ Sauce (page 220)

Place the pork shoulder in a large mixing bowl. Pour the vinegar over the shoulder. Cover and refrigerate 2 hours, turning every 30 minutes to evenly coat the meat with the vinegar. Remove the pork from the bowl and discard the vinegar. Pat the surface of the shoulder dry.

Combine the seasonings and rub over the entire surface of the shoulder. Lightly cover and refrigerate overnight.

Soak the wood chips in water for 2–3 hours.

Prepare the grill. Grill the pork over indirect medium heat until the internal temperature reaches 185–190 degrees, 4–4½ hours. Turn the pork every 30–40 minutes. Add small amounts of wood chips to the coals to keep smoke going while cooking.

Using 2 forks, pull the pork into shreds and discard any large pieces of fat.

Combine the pork with the barbeque sauce, and keep warm until ready to serve.

YIELD: 8–10 servings

# Molasses-Glazed Ham Steaks

If you can find sorghum, feel free to substitute it for the molasses, giving the dish more depth. Good for a Saturday afternoon brunch, served with grilled potato salad and grilled asparagus.

¾ cup orange juice

½ cup molasses

1 tsp garlic powder

1 tsp onion powder

1 tsp crushed red pepper flakes

1 tsp Worcestershire sauce

Two 1-lb bone-in ham steaks

In a saucepan over low heat, cook the orange juice slightly and then whisk in the remaining ingredients except the ham steaks.

Place the ham steaks in a Baggie and pour in the marinade. Seal the Baggie and refrigerate the ham for 2–3 hours, turning once or twice to make sure all surfaces are covered. Remove the steaks from the refrigerator 1 hour before grilling.

Remove the steaks from the marinade and pour the remaining marinade into a small sauce pot. Place the liquid over medium heat and simmer until reduced by half.

Using a small paring knife, make small slits through the fat on the outer perimeter of the ham steaks. Grill over direct medium heat until the ham turns brown and crispy. Turn once while cooking. While the ham is grilling, brush the surfaces with the reduced marinade. Remove the ham from the grill and cut into serving-sized pieces, and drizzle with any remaining marinade.

YIELD: 6–8 servings

# Dr Pepper-Glazed Ham

You may never eat another non-soft-drink-glazed ham again. Well worth the time and effort; great for holiday gift-giving. If you don't have an aluminum disposable roasting pan, use a roasting pan that has been completely lined with foil.

4 cups wood chips

24 oz Dr Pepper

2 Tbl mayhaw jelly (or muscadine jelly)

2 bay leaves

2 Tbl Pickapeppa sauce

1 tsp minced garlic

2 Tbl minced shallots

5 whole cloves

1 cinnamon stick

1 Tbl fresh orange zest

¼ cup freshly squeezed orange juice

2 tsp lemon zest

2 tsp lime zest

1 cured smoked ham, 10–12 lbs

1 tsp dry mustard

1 cup light brown sugar

Prepare grill for low heat cooking and soak 4 cups of wood chips.

Combine all ingredients for the glaze in a small sauce pot.

Place over medium heat and simmer 30 minutes. Strain the liquid and discard the solids. Return the mixture to the stove and reduce to ¾ cup liquid.

Place the ham on a V-shaped baking rack in a disposable roasting pan. Using a paring knife, cut shallow slits in a criss-cross pattern on the top of the ham. Spoon 2 tablespoons of the glaze over the top of the ham.

Combine the dry mustard and brown sugar, and press the mixture over the entire surface of the ham. Pour 1 cup of water into the bottom of the roasting pan.

Prepare the grill or smoker. Add wood chips to the charcoal as needed. Cook over indirect medium heat to an internal temperature of 165 degrees. Spoon 1–2 tablespoons of the glaze over the ham every 15–20 minutes until all of the glaze is gone. Cover as much of the surface of the ham as possible.

Allow the ham to rest for 20–30 minutes before carving.

YIELD: 10–14 servings

# Pork Tenderloin Wrapped in Bacon with Blackberry Chutney

Thick bacon doesn't work with this recipe. If blackberries are out of season, feel free to substitute the frozen variety. The chutney is best when made a few days in advance and kept chilled. It holds for one week in the refrigerator.

1 cup apple juice

1 Tbl balsamic vinegar

1 bay leaf

2 Tbl brown sugar

⅛ tsp cinnamon

¼ tsp freshly ground black pepper

1 tsp kosher salt

2 whole pork tenderloins, cleaned and trimmed

8–10 slices thin-cut bacon

1 recipe Blackberry Chutney (recipe follows)

Combine the apple juice, vinegar, bay leaf, brown sugar, cinnamon, pepper, and salt in a small sauce pot, and heat just long enough to melt the sugar. Allow to cool.

Place the tenderloins in a Ziploc bag and pour the cooled marinade over the pork. Close the bag and marinate the pork 2–3 hours, turning several times to ensure that all surfaces are covered.

Remove the pork from the marinade and pat dry. Starting at one end of the tenderloin, firmly wrap the bacon around the meat in a spiral direction, making sure to cover all surface areas of the pork.

Prepare the grill. Sear the pork for 8 minutes over medium direct heat, turning it one quarter turn every 2–3 minutes. Continue cooking with medium indirect heat until the pork reaches an internal temperature of 165 degrees, 15–20 minutes.

Remove the pork from the grill and let rest 5 minutes. Slice the pork on a slight angle into 1-inch-thick slices and serve with Blackberry Chutney.

YIELD: 6–8 portions

(continued)

# Blackberry Chutney

1 cup finely chopped shallots

1 cup medium dice onions

1 Tbl unsalted butter

2 cups blackberries

¼ cup sugar

½ cup blackberry preserves

2 Tbl cider vinegar

1 Tbl cracked black pepper

1 Tbl minced ginger

1 cinnamon stick

½ tsp Creole Seasoning
    (page 212)

In a 1½-quart heavy-duty saucepan, cook shallots and onions in butter over moderate heat, stirring occasionally, until golden, 3–5 minutes. Stir in remaining ingredients and simmer, uncovered, stirring occasionally, until berries burst and chutney is thickened, approximately 20 minutes. Strain through a fine mesh sieve to remove seeds.

Cool to room temperature.

YIELD: 2 cups

*"The chutney is best when made a few days in advance and kept chilled. It holds for one week in the refrigerator."*

# Whole Grilled Tenderloin with Chive-Tarragon Mayonnaise

I love the French classic béarnaise sauce when served with beef. The New Orleans restaurants of my youth all served béarnaise. This is a great way to offer similar flavor profiles without having to make a complicated and heat-sensitive emulsification. The sauce is stable and travels well in a cooler. When using fresh tarragon, double the amount. This is a great dish to bring to a friend's home. To crack black peppercorns, place the peppercorns on a cutting board and place the palm of your hand in the bottom of a small skillet. Move the skillet bottom back and forth over the peppercorns to break them into tiny, irregular pieces.

Center-cut beef tenderloin, 3½–4 lbs

1½ Tbl Steak Seasoning (page 211)

2 Tbl freshly cracked black pepper

1 recipe Chive-Tarragon Mayonnaise (recipe follows)

Coat the surface of the tenderloin with the Steak Seasoning and cracked black pepper. Allow seasoned tenderloin to sit at room temperature 1 hour before grilling.

Sear tenderloin over medium direct heat until it is well marked, about 15 minutes, turning one quarter of a turn every 4–5 minutes. Continue cooking over medium indirect heat until desired doneness is reached, 15–20 minutes for medium rare.

Remove from the grill and allow tenderloin to rest for 6–7 minutes before slicing.

Slice the tenderloin into ½-inch-thick slices and serve with Chive-Tarragon Mayonnaise on the side.

YIELD: 10–12 portions

(continued)

# Chive-Tarragon Mayonnaise

½ cup red wine vinegar

½ cup white wine

2 Tbl orange juice

3 Tbl minced shallots

1 tsp minced fresh garlic

3 Tbl dried tarragon

2 egg yolks

2 tsp Dijon mustard

1 tsp kosher salt

1½ cups canola oil

Warm water as needed

½ tsp freshly ground black pepper

¼ cup thinly sliced fresh chives

This chive and tarragon mayo is also an excellent condiment with burgers and roast beef sandwiches.

Place vinegar, wine, orange juice, shallots, garlic, and tarragon in a small sauté pan. Simmer over medium heat until mixture has reduced by 75 percent. Remove from the heat and cool.

Place the egg yolks, mustard, and salt in a stainless-steel mixing bowl. Beat with a wire whisk for 2–3 minutes. Add in half of the tarragon reduction and slowly begin drizzling in the oil, constantly whipping the mixture. As the mayonnaise begins to thicken, add the remaining tarragon reduction, and continue to whisk in the oil. If the mixture becomes too thick, add 1–2 teaspoons of warm water.

Add pepper and chives, and store refrigerated until needed.

YIELD: 2 cups

*"I love the French classic béarnaise sauce when served with beef. The New Orleans restaurants of my youth all served béarnaise."*

# Cracked Pepper Filet with Mustard Cognac Sauce

A simplified version of the French classic au poivre. Experiment with different mustard. Creole or your favorite whole-grain mustard would be nice substitutions.

Six 6–8-ounce filets mignons

2 Tbl No-stick Grilling Marinade for Beef (page 205)

1 Tbl kosher salt

½ cup cracked black pepper

Lightly brush the surfaces of the filets mignons with the marinade and set aside for 45 minutes. The steaks should remain out at room temperature while they marinate.

Season the marinated steaks with the salt and firmly press the black pepper onto the surfaces of the steaks.

Cook the steaks on direct high heat to your desired doneness, 8–10 minutes for medium rare. Turn the steaks once while cooking.

Top each cooked steak with 1–2 ounces of Mustard Cognac Sauce (recipe follows).

YIELD: 6 servings

## Mustard Cognac Sauce

2 tsp olive oil

½ tsp minced fresh garlic

1 Tbl minced shallots

¼ tsp salt

¼ cup cognac

2 Tbl brown sugar

½ cup Veal Stock (recipe follows)

1 cup whipping cream

2 Tbl Dijon mustard

Heat the olive oil in a small sauté pan over low heat. Add the garlic, shallots, and salt and cook 3–4 minutes, stirring often. Add the cognac and brown sugar and cook 5–6 minutes until the mixture looks like a thick syrup.

Add the Veal Stock and cook until the mixture has reduced by half. Add the cream and cook until the sauce has again reduced by half. Remove from the heat and stir in the mustard.

YIELD: 2 cups

(continued)

# Veal Stock

4 pounds veal bones

1 gallon cold water

1 pound yellow onions, cut
  into large pieces

¾ pound carrots, peeled and
  cut into large pieces

½ pound celery, cleaned and
  cut into large pieces

3 bay leaves

½ bunch fresh parsley

4–6 sprigs of fresh thyme

3 peeled garlic cloves, smashed

½ Tbl cracked black
  peppercorns

Rinse the veal bones under cold water for 4–5 minutes. Place
the bones in a large stockpot, and cover them with the water.
Place over low medium heat and slowly bring to a simmer.

Using a ladle, skim off any gray foam that floats to the top
and allow the stock to come to a very slow simmer with tiny
little bubbles gently rising to the surface. Set a timer for
6 hours. Keep an eye on the stock and add more water as the
stock reduces.

After 6 hours, skim the stock to remove fat and scum, and then
add the remaining ingredients. Top off the stock with water
again and allow to cook 12–14 hours maintaining a steady
slow simmer.

When the timer goes off, strain the stock and discard all
bones and vegetables. Fill sink with heavily iced water and
place the container of stock in the ice bath to cool as quickly
as possible. Once stock is completely cooled, remove any
fat from the surface.

YIELD: 3 quarts

# Grilled Porterhouse Steaks with Deep South Steak Sauce

The beauty of a porterhouse is that you get to eat a strip and a filet, though the filet side cooks faster than the strip. To get an evenly cooked steak, make sure that the filet side is to the outer edge of the grill where the coals are cooler.

6 porterhouse steaks,
  14–16 oz each

⅓ cup No-stick Grilling
  Marinade for Beef
  (page 205)

1½ Tbl kosher salt

1 Tbl freshly ground black
  pepper

1 recipe Deep South Steak
  Sauce (page 228)

Brush the steaks with the marinade. Refrigerate the steaks for 1 hour. Remove the steaks from the refrigerator, and allow them to marinate for another hour at room temperature. Sprinkle the steaks with the salt and pepper. Grill over direct high heat until desired doneness is reached, 10–12 minutes for medium rare. Remove the steaks from the grill, and allow them to rest for 5 minutes before serving.

Serve with Deep South Steak Sauce on the side.

YIELD: **6 servings**

# Cowboy Ribeyes with Tobacco Onions and a Roasted Garlic Bordelaise

Bone-in steaks offer more flavor and they make your dog happy, too. Use the Roasted Garlic Bordelaise with filet mignon on potato cakes for an upscale treat, or top a hamburger steak for a more casual alternative.

6 bone-in ribeye steaks,
   1–1¼ lbs each

⅓ cup No-stick Grilling
   Marinade for Beef
   (page 205)

2 Tbl kosher salt

2 tsp Steak Seasoning
   (page 211)

1 Tbl freshly ground black
   pepper

1 recipe Tobacco Onions
   (page 91)

1 recipe Roasted Garlic
   Bordelaise (page 216)

Brush steaks with the marinade and allow them to marinate at room temperature for 45 minutes. Combine the salt, Steak Seasoning, and black pepper, and season the steaks.

Prepare grill and cook over direct high heat until desired doneness is reached, 8–10 minutes for medium rare. Turn the steaks once while cooking. If flare-ups occur, move the steaks to indirect heat for a minute or two.

Remove the steaks from the grill and allow them to rest for 5 minutes before serving.

To serve, place a small mound of Tobacco Onions on each serving dish, rest the steaks on the onions, and top with the Roasted Garlic Bordelaise.

YIELD: 6 servings

# Whole Smoked Prime Rib

I had my friend and devout carnivore, Ronnie Kent, try this finished recipe. On a scale from 1 to 10, he gave it an 11. When chilled and sliced thin, it makes a great salad. Use the leftover prime rib, shaved thin, for an incredible Philly cheesesteak sandwich.

1 boneless rib roast, 5–6 lbs

½ cup No-stick Grilling Marinade for Beef (page 205)

2 Tbl kosher salt

1 Tbl freshly ground black pepper

Trim any excess fat from the rib roast.

Brush the marinade over the surface of the rib roast, and allow it to marinate at room temperature for 1 hour.

Prepare grill for medium-indirect-heat cooking.

Sprinkle roast with salt and pepper. Place the roast on the grill, fat side up, and cook to desired doneness, 1½–2 hours for medium rare. Use a meat thermometer to check temperature (135–140 degrees for medium rare).

Transfer the roast to a cutting board and cover it with foil. Allow the roast to rest for 15 minutes before carving.

YIELD: 8–10 servings

# Carpetbagger Strips with Andouille Stuffing

Carpetbagger steaks are always a hit in our restaurants. Feel free to improvise and add any additional ingredients that you think would be good accompaniments.

6 New York strip steaks,
    8–10 oz each

¼ cup No-stick Grilling
    Marinade for Beef
    (page 205)

2 Tbl Steak Seasoning
    (page 211)

1 recipe Andouille Stuffing
    (recipe follows)

Brush the steaks with the marinade and let sit at room temperature for 15–20 minutes. Sprinkle both sides of the steaks with the Steak Seasoning. Grill over direct high heat until desired doneness is reached, 8–10 minutes for medium rare. Remove steaks from the grill and allow to rest 5 minutes. Using a sharp knife, butterfly the steak from the outer edge along the center, forming a pocket. Fill the pocket with the Andouille Stuffing, allowing some to spill out onto the plate. Serve immediately.

YIELD: **6 servings**

## Andouille Stuffing

1 Tbl bacon fat or canola oil

¾ lb andouille sausage,
    medium dice

1 cup small dice onions

½ cup medium dice green bell
    peppers

¼ cup small dice red bell
    peppers

1 Tbl minced garlic

2 tsp crushed red pepper flakes

½ cup Veal Stock (page 158)

¼ cup unsalted butter, cut
    into cubes

2 tsp kosher salt

Melt the bacon fat in a large sauté pan over high heat. Brown the andouille sausage and drain most of the excess fat. Lower heat to medium and add the onions, green and red peppers, and garlic, and cook 6–7 minutes more. Add the crushed red pepper flakes and Veal Stock. Bring the mixture to a simmer. Begin adding the butter cubes, a few at a time, stirring constantly with a wire whisk. Once all the butter has been incorporated, add the salt and remove the stuffing from the heat. Hold in a warm place until ready to fill steaks.

YIELD: **6 servings**

# Carpetbagger Strips with Shrimp Stuffing

Surf and turf all in one dish. If you have pesto hanging around in the refrigerator or freezer, add it in lieu of fresh basil.

6 New York steaks,
    8–10 oz each

¼ cup No-stick Grilling
    Marinade for Beef
    (page 205)

2 Tbl Steak Seasoning
    (page 211)

1 recipe Shrimp Stuffing
    (recipe follows)

Brush the steaks with the marinade and let sit at room temperature for 15–20 minutes. Sprinkle both sides of the steaks with the Steak Seasoning. Grill over direct high heat until desired doneness is reached, 8–10 minutes for medium rare. Remove steaks from the grill and allow to rest 5 minutes. Using a sharp knife, butterfly the steak from the outer edge along the center, forming a pocket. Fill the pocket with the Shrimp Stuffing, allowing some to spill out onto the plate. Serve immediately.

YIELD: **6 servings**

# Shrimp Stuffing

¼ cup olive oil

½ lb small fresh shrimp

2 tsp Old Bay seasoning

½ cup small dice yellow onions

1 tsp minced garlic

2 cups shiitake mushrooms, stems removed and sliced thin

¾ cup small dice celery

½ cup white wine

1 Tbl fresh orange juice

1 Tbl white vinegar

1 cup medium dice fresh tomatoes, seeds removed

1 cup whipping cream

1 Tbl chopped fresh basil

1 tsp freshly ground black pepper

Heat olive oil in a large sauté pan over high heat. Season shrimp with the Old Bay seasoning and sauté in hot oil for 3 minutes. Add onion, garlic, mushrooms, and celery, and cook 3–4 minutes more. Deglaze with white wine, add orange juice and vinegar, and allow it to reduce by half. Add tomatoes and cream, and cook until the sauce becomes thick enough to coat the back of a spoon. Stir in the basil and black pepper, and remove from heat. Keep warm until ready to fill steaks.

YIELD: **6 servings**

*"Surf and turf all in one dish."*

# Carpetbagger Strips with Crabmeat Stuffing

Fresh Gulf crabmeat is one of life's greatest culinary pleasures. When paired with beef, it takes on a new dimension. Shiitake mushrooms can be substituted to add a bolder flavor profile.

6 New York steaks, 8–10 oz each

¼ cup No-stick Grilling Marinade for Beef (page 205)

2 Tbl Steak Seasoning (page 211)

1 recipe Crabmeat Stuffing (recipe follows)

Brush the steaks with the marinade and let sit at room temperature for 15–20 minutes. Sprinkle both sides of the steaks with the Steak Seasoning. Grill over direct high heat until desired doneness is reached, 8–10 minutes for medium rare. Remove steaks from the grill and allow to rest 5 minutes. Using a sharp knife, butterfly the steak from the outer edge along the center, forming a pocket. Fill the pocket with the Crabmeat Stuffing, allowing some to spill out onto the plate. Serve immediately.

YIELD: 6 servings

## Crabmeat Stuffing

1 Tbl olive oil

½ cup thinly sliced shallots

2 cups thinly sliced button mushrooms

⅓ cup julienned green bell peppers

1 tsp Creole Seasoning (page 212)

½ tsp kosher salt

½ cup white wine

1 Tbl fresh lemon juice

¾ cup thinly sliced green onions

1 cup unsalted butter, cut into cubes

¾ lb all lump crabmeat

Heat olive oil in a large sauté pan over medium heat. Sauté shallots, mushrooms, green bell peppers, Creole Seasoning, and salt for 8–10 minutes. Add wine and lemon juice, and allow liquid to reduce by half. Stir in the green onions. Start adding butter cubes, a few at a time, while stirring constantly with a wire whisk. Once all of the butter has been incorporated, gently fold in the crabmeat. Keep warm until ready to fill the steaks.

YIELD: 6 servings

# Carpetbagger Steaks with Oyster Stuffing

If you have time, smoke the oysters first before adding them to the stuffing mixture for another flavor dimension.

6 New York steaks, 8–10 oz each

¼ cup No-stick Grilling Marinade for Beef (page 205)

2 Tbl Steak Seasoning (page 211)

1 recipe Oyster Stuffing (recipe follows)

Brush the steaks with the marinade and let sit at room temperature for 15–20 minutes. Sprinkle both sides of the steaks with the Steak Seasoning. Grill over direct high heat until desired doneness is reached, 8–10 minutes for medium rare. Remove steaks from the grill and allow to rest 5 minutes. Using a sharp knife, butterfly the steak from the outer edge along the center, forming a pocket. Fill the pocket with the Oyster Stuffing, allowing some to spill out onto the plate. Serve immediately.

YIELD: 6 servings

## Oyster Stuffing

1 Tbl olive oil

¼ cup small dice bacon

½ cup small dice shallots

1½ cups drained and roughly chopped artichoke hearts

1 cup shucked oysters, drained

½ cup white wine

½ cup thinly sliced green onions

1 tsp chopped fresh thyme

1 cup Parmesan Cream Sauce (page 129)

1 tsp kosher salt

1 tsp freshly ground black pepper

Heat olive oil over medium heat. Place diced bacon in hot oil, and cook bacon until it browns and just starts to become crispy. Drain excess fat, leaving just enough to coat the bottom of the sauté pan. Add shallots, artichoke hearts, and oysters, and cook until the edges of the oysters begin to curl. Deglaze with wine, add green onions and thyme, and simmer for 2 minutes. Add Parmesan Cream Sauce and simmer until sauce is thick enough to coat the back of a spoon. Add salt and pepper, and remove from the heat. Store warm until ready to fill the steaks.

YIELD: 6 servings

# Andouille-Stuffed Prime Rib

A long, sharp knife is a must when stuffing the prime rib. Be careful not to cut all of the way through, but if you do, continue to fill the center of the roast, then tie the entire roast with butcher's twine.

1 Tbl bacon fat or canola oil

½ pound andouille sausage, ½-inch dice

½ cup small dice yellow onions

½ cup small dice celery

¼ cup small dice red bell peppers

1 cup diced button mushrooms

1 Tbl minced fresh garlic

2 tsp Creole Seasoning (page 212)

2 tsp freshly ground black pepper

½ tsp dried basil

1 egg, slightly beaten

½ cup panko, Japanese bread crumbs

1 prime rib roast, 4–4½ lbs

¼ cup olive oil

1½ Tbl Steak Seasoning (page 211)

Heat the bacon fat in a large sauté pan over high heat. Brown the andouille sausage in the hot fat. Drain excess fat, leaving approximately 1 tablespoon in the pan. Reduce heat to medium and add onions, celery, red bell peppers, and mushrooms. Cook 6–8 minutes, stirring occasionally. Add garlic, Creole Seasoning, 1 teaspoon black pepper, and basil; cook 2–3 minutes more. Remove mixture from the heat and place in a large mixing bowl. Allow mixture to cool completely. Once cooled, add egg and bread crumbs.

To stuff the prime rib: Trim excess fat from the prime rib. Using a long narrow knife, bore a hole, approximately 3 inches wide, in the center of the prime rib that runs the length of the meat. Fill the hole with the andouille mixture by stuffing the prime rib from both ends. Allow the roast to sit at room temperature for 1 hour before cooking.

Brush the outside of the prime rib with the olive oil and season with the Steak Seasoning and 1 tablespoon black pepper.

Preheat the grill. Sear prime rib on direct high heat for 20 minutes, turning once. Transfer to indirect high heat and continue cooking until desired doneness is reached, approximately 1¼ hours for medium rare.

Allow the prime rib to rest for 15 minutes before slicing and serving.

Cut into 1-inch-thick slices and serve.

YIELD: 6–8 servings

# Tenderloin with Sizzling Butter

Beef and butter . . . check your cholesterol count at the door.

1 center-cut beef tenderloin,
  3½–4 lbs

1 cup Creamy Balsamic
  Vinaigrette Dressing
  (page 74)

2 tsp Creole Seasoning
  (page 212)

1 tsp Steak Seasoning
  (page 211)

2 tsp freshly ground black
  pepper

1 cup Clarified Butter
  (page 218)

Trim excess fat from tenderloin. Place tenderloin in a large
Ziploc bag and pour the Creamy Balsamic Vinaigrette Dressing
into the bag with the beef. Marinate in refrigerator for 5–6
hours. Occasionally shake the bag to ensure that all of the
beef is covered with the marinade.

Remove marinated beef from the bag and blot it dry using
paper towels. Season the surface of the tenderloin with Creole
Seasoning, Steak Seasoning, and the black pepper.

Prepare grill. Sear tenderloin over medium heat until it is
well marked, about 15 minutes, turning one quarter of a turn
every 4–5 minutes. Remove from direct heat and continue
cooking until desired doneness is reached, 15–20 minutes for
medium rare.

Remove from grill and allow tenderloin to rest for 6–7 minutes
before slicing. Slice tenderloin into ¼-inch-thick slices.

Just before serving, heat the Clarified Butter in a skillet until
it begins to bubble. Drizzle over the sliced meat and serve
immediately.

**YIELD: 6–8 servings**

# Grilled Stuffed Tenderloin

Be careful when running the knife through the center of the tenderloin. Keep it in the center. You can use a handheld sharpening steel to bore the hole out a little larger. Be firm, but don't over-force the stuffing when filling the tenderloin.

2 Tbl olive oil

¼ cup minced shallots

1 Tbl minced garlic

2 tsp kosher salt

1 tsp freshly ground black
    pepper

¾ lb fresh spinach, cleaned and
    stems removed

¼ cup roasted and peeled small
    dice red bell peppers

¼ cup chopped fresh basil

¼ pound Gorgonzola cheese,
    crumbled

1 center-cut beef tenderloin,
    3½ –4 lbs

2 Tbl Steak Seasoning
    (page 211)

Heat olive oil in a large sauté pan over medium heat. Cook shallots, garlic, salt, and pepper for 3–4 minutes; do not brown. Add spinach and cook until the spinach is wilted, 1–2 minutes, stirring constantly.

Drain excess moisture and place spinach in a mixing bowl. Add roasted red bell peppers, basil, and Gorgonzola.

Using a long narrow knife, make a hole tunneling through the center of the tenderloin and running the length of the meat. While the knife is still inserted in the beef, rotate it one full turn to create a larger opening. Fill the hole with the spinach mixture by stuffing the tenderloin from both ends. Use a wooden spoon to push the filling toward the center of the tenderloin.

Sprinkle the entire surface of the tenderloin with Steak Seasoning.

Prepare grill and sear tenderloin over direct medium heat for 15 minutes, turning one-quarter turn every 4–5 minutes during the searing process.

Once seared, move the tenderloin to cook over indirect heat until desired doneness is reached, 20–30 minutes for medium rare. Turn the tenderloin once every 15 minutes during this stage. Remove the tenderloin from the grill and allow to rest for 5–10 minutes before carving. Carefully cut tenderloin into 1-inch-thick slices and serve.

YIELD: **6 servings**

# Marinated Ribeye Steaks

The ribeye is my favorite cut of beef. It is also the easiest and best of the typical steak cuts to marinate. I like my steaks highly seasoned, and this is a great way to accomplish that without piling on additional powdered seasonings.

6 ribeye steaks, 10–12 oz each

3 Tbl lemon pepper seasoning

1 cup soy sauce

1 Tbl onion powder

1 Tbl garlic powder

1 Tbl sugar

1 tsp dry ginger

1 tsp paprika

2 Tbl minced garlic

2 Tbl Liquid Smoke

2 Tbl Steak Seasoning
   (page 211)

Mix all ingredients except the Steak Seasoning together in a bowl. Place the steaks in a gallon-sized Ziploc bag (no more than 2 steaks per bag) and pour enough marinade into the bag to cover the steaks halfway when they are lying flat. Squeeze all excess air out of the bag and seal. Allow the steaks to marinate in the refrigerator, lying flat, for no longer than 2 hours. Remove steaks from refrigerator 30 minutes before grilling.

Sprinkle the ribeyes with the Steak Seasoning.

Prepare grill and cook steaks over direct high heat, cooking until desired doneness is reached, 10–12 minutes for medium rare. Turn the steaks once during cooking.

YIELD: **6 servings**

Stuffnsuch

# Marinated Beef and Chicken Fajitas with Smoky Fajita Sauce

This is the perfect by-the-pool summer entrée. Great for company. The soy-pineapple marinade tenderizes the meat, but don't overmarinate or the finished product will be dry. We tested with Anaheim chilies, but any mild- to medium-heat peppers may be substituted. A grill topper will be needed for this recipe.

1 cup soy sauce

1 cup pineapple juice

1 flank steak, about 1 lb and ¾ inch thick

1 lb boneless, skinless chicken breasts

2 tsp paprika

2 tsp brown sugar

3 tsp chili powder

1 tsp cumin

1 tsp dry oregano

1 tsp coriander

⅛ tsp cinnamon

1 Tbl plus 2 tsp kosher salt

1 Tbl freshly ground black pepper

1 red bell pepper, seeds removed and julienned

2 Anaheim chilies, seeds removed and julienned

2 yellow wax peppers, seeds removed and julienned

1 medium red onion, peeled and cut into ½-inch-thick strips

2 Tbl olive oil

Eighteen 6-inch flour tortillas

Smoky Fajita Sauce (page 229)

2 cups shredded lettuce

1 cup diced tomatoes

¼ cup chiffonaded cilantro

1 cup salsa

Combine the soy sauce and pineapple juice and divide the marinade between 2 gallon-sized Ziploc bags. Place the flank steak in one bag and the chicken in another. After 30 minutes, remove the steak and chicken from the marinade. Pat the surfaces of the meat dry.

Combine the paprika, brown sugar, chili powder, cumin, oregano, coriander, cinnamon, 1 tablespoon salt, and pepper in a small dish. Use this mixture to liberally season the surface of the steak and chicken.

Prepare the grill. Cook both the steak and chicken over direct high heat for 8–10 minutes. Remove the meat from the grill

(continued)

and allow to rest for 8–10 minutes. While the meat is resting, toss the onion and peppers in the olive oil.

Place a grill screen on high heat and allow it to get very hot. Spread the pepper mixture onto the grill topper and sprinkle it with the 2 teaspoons salt. Cook for 6–8 minutes, turning the vegetables once.

Wrap the tortillas—in packages of three—in aluminum foil. Place the wrapped tortillas over medium direct heat for 3–4 minutes, turning once. Hold the tortillas and vegetables in a warm place.

Use a sharp knife to cut the flank steak, against the grain, into ¼-inch-thick slices. Cut the chicken into ¼-inch-thick long strips.

Place the chicken, beef, and peppers on a serving dish and serve the tortillas on the side with Smoky Fajita Sauce, shredded lettuce, diced tomatoes, cilantro, and your favorite salsa.

YIELD: 6–8 servings

*"This is the perfect by-the-pool summer entrée. Great for company."*

# Grilled Leg of Lamb with Raspberry Mint Sauce

Whole bone-in leg of lamb may be substituted, but use medium indirect heat for two hours. Mint is the perfect accompaniment for lamb, and raspberries are the perfect accompaniment for mint. Use fresh raspberries when available, but frozen may be substituted.

½ cup Roasted Garlic Puree
   (page 42)

¼ cup olive oil

1 Tbl chopped fresh rosemary

¼ cup chopped fresh mint

2 Tbl sherry vinegar

1 boneless leg of lamb,
   3–3½ lbs, butterflied

2 Tbl kosher salt

1 Tbl freshly ground black
   pepper

1 recipe Raspberry Mint Sauce
   (recipe follows)

Place the garlic, oil, rosemary, mint, and vinegar in a mixing bowl. Blend together using a wire whisk.

Trim any excess fat and sinew from the lamb. Lay the lamb on a flat surface, and spread half of the garlic mixture over it. Roll the lamb tightly into a cylinder. Tie the lamb with butcher's twine so that it maintains the cylinder shape. Rub the outside of the lamb with the remaining garlic mixture, and sprinkle the surface with the salt and pepper. Allow the lamb to sit at room temperature 30–40 minutes before grilling.

Prepare the grill. Sear the lamb for 15–20 minutes over medium direct heat, turning every 3–4 minutes. Once the lamb has browned on all sides, continue cooking over medium indirect heat until the lamb has reached desired doneness, approximately 1 hour and 15 minutes for medium rare. Remove the lamb from the grill and let rest 15 minutes before carving. Cut away the twine. Using a carving knife, cut lamb against the grain into ¼-inch-thick slices.

Serve with Raspberry Mint Sauce.

YIELD: 10–12 servings

(continued)

# Raspberry Mint Sauce

3 Tbl olive oil

2 Tbl minced shallots

1 cup raspberries

½ cup sugar

1 cup red wine

1½ cups Veal Stock (page 158)

3 Tbl cold unsalted butter, cut
    into small cubes

½ tsp kosher salt

1 Tbl chopped fresh mint

In a saucepan over medium heat, combine oil, shallots, raspberries, sugar, and red wine and simmer until most of the liquid is gone. Purée mixture and pass through a fine mesh strainer.

Return the strained mixture to a small sauce pot and add the Veal Stock. Bring the mixture to a simmer. Add the butter cubes while whisking briskly. Stir until all of the butter is incorporated. Remove the sauce from the heat, and add salt and mint. Store in a warm place until needed.

YIELD: **2 cups**

# Grilled Lamb Chops with Roasted Garlic-Mint Compound Butter

Make all of the components ahead of time and grill the chops at the last minute.

4 racks of lamb, cut into 16 double-bone chops

⅓ cup No-stick Grilling Marinade for Beef (page 205)

1 Tbl kosher salt

1 tsp freshly ground black pepper

1 recipe Roasted Garlic–Mint Compound Butter (recipe follows)

Coat the surface of the lamb chops with the marinade. Marinate at room temperature 30 minutes. Sprinkle the chops with the salt and pepper.

Prepare the grill. Cook over direct medium heat until desired doneness is reached, 12–14 minutes for medium rare. Remove from the grill and place on serving dishes. Top each chop with a rosette of Roasted Garlic–Mint Compound Butter and serve immediately.

YIELD: 8 servings

(continued)

# Roasted Garlic-Mint Compound Butter

1 tsp olive oil

2 tsp minced shallots

½ cup Roasted Garlic Puree
  (page 42)

1 tsp kosher salt

2 Tbl Riesling wine

½ tsp freshly ground black
  pepper

1 Tbl mint jelly

2 Tbl finely chopped
  fresh mint

¾ cup unsalted butter, softened

1 tsp Worcestershire sauce

½ tsp hot sauce

In a small sauté pan, heat the oil over low heat. Cook the shallots, garlic, and salt 3–4 minutes. Add the wine, pepper, and mint jelly and cook 5 minutes more, stirring often to prevent sticking and burning. Add the mint and cook for 1 minute more. Remove from the heat and cool completely.

Place the softened butter in a mixing bowl. Using a rubber spatula, blend together all of the ingredients.

Line a large platter or small baking sheet with waxed paper. Place the butter in a pastry bag with a medium star tip attached. Pipe rosettes—2–3 teaspoons each—onto the waxed paper. You should have 16 rosettes when finished. Refrigerate until needed.

YIELD: 16 rosettes

# Smoked Beef Brisket

As an alternative, smoke the brisket for 3 hours and then finish it in a 180-degree oven for 5 hours.

1 beef brisket, 7–8 lbs

1 cup white vinegar

½ cup paprika

¼ cup garlic powder

2 Tbl onion powder

1 Tbl freshly ground black
    pepper

2 Tbl kosher salt

¼ cup brown sugar

⅓ cup sugar

1 Tbl Creole Seasoning
    (page 212)

6–8 cups wood chips

1 recipe BBQ Sauce
    (page 220)

Place the brisket in a roasting pan. Pour vinegar over the brisket. Cover and refrigerate for 2 hours, turning every 30 minutes to evenly coat the meat with the vinegar. Remove the pork from the bowl and discard the vinegar. Pat the surface of the brisket dry.

Combine the paprika, garlic powder, onion powder, black pepper, salt, brown sugar, sugar, and Creole Seasoning, and rub over the entire surface of the brisket. Lightly cover and refrigerate overnight.

Soak the wood chips in water 2–3 hours. Drain well.

Prepare the grill. Sprinkle a small handful of chips over the prepared charcoal. Place the brisket back in a V-shaped baking rack in a roasting pan, and cook over indirect low heat until the internal temperature reaches 190 degrees.

While the brisket is cooking, use a pastry brush to baste it with any juices that collect in the roasting pan. The brisket will take 7–8 hours to cook. Add charcoal every 30–40 minutes, and add wood chips to the coals as needed to keep the smoke billowing.

Remove brisket and let sit for 15–20 minutes. Slice thin and serve with BBQ Sauce on the side.

YIELD: 8–12 servings

# Grilled Stuffed Peppers

My mom made great stuffed peppers. A basic and good recipe, they were my annually requested birthday meal. I don't like rice in my stuffed peppers, but if you must, try using leftover dirty rice for an added dimension.

1 Tbl bacon fat

1 cup small dice yellow onions

1 tsp Steak Seasoning (page 211)

1 tsp kosher salt

2 Tbl sugar

1 tsp freshly ground black pepper

2 tsp finely minced fresh garlic

¼ tsp dry basil

¼ tsp dry oregano

⅛ tsp dry thyme

2 Tbl tomato paste

1 egg, slightly beaten

1½ lbs lean ground beef

One 28-ounce can diced tomatoes, drained very well

6 large bell peppers, tops and seeds removed

In a small sauté pan, heat the bacon fat over medium heat. Add onions, Steak Seasoning, salt, sugar, and pepper, and cook 3–4 minutes. Add the garlic, basil, oregano, and thyme, and cook 1 minute more. Stir in the tomato paste and cook 4–5 minutes, stirring constantly.

Remove mixture from the heat and transfer to a large mixing bowl. Allow to cool completely.

Once the mixture has cooled, mix in the egg, ground beef, and drained tomatoes. Fill each pepper with the ground beef mixture.

Prepare the grill. Cook the peppers over indirect medium heat for 20–25 minutes.

Remove from the grill and serve.

YIELD: 6 servings

# Grilled Focaccia

This recipe must be carefully cooked over medium low heat. Make the Basil Tapenade recipe (page 24), and dip the focaccia into it.

1 Tbl honey

2 packages active dry yeast

1⅓ cups warm water
   (110 degrees)

4 cups all-purpose flour

1 tsp salt

¼ cup plus 2 Tbl olive oil

2 tsp kosher salt

1 tsp freshly ground black
   pepper

2 tsp chopped fresh rosemary

In a small bowl, combine the honey, yeast, and half of the warm water. Mix well and let stand until the mixture looks creamy, about 10 minutes.

Place the flour and salt in a large mixing bowl. Add the yeast mixture and begin mixing, either by hand or using the dough hook attachment of an electric mixer. Add in the remaining water, a few tablespoons at a time, and the 2 tablespoons of olive oil. Continue kneading until the dough begins to pull away from the sides of the bowl. Turn the dough out onto a lightly floured surface and knead for 2–3 minutes more.

Lightly oil a large mixing bowl. Place the dough in the bowl and turn once to coat with oil. Cover with a damp cloth and place in a warm place. Allow the dough to rise until doubled in size, about 30 minutes.

Deflate the dough and roll it out to a ½-inch thickness on a lightly floured surface.

Brush the dough with the remaining olive oil, and sprinkle with the salt, pepper, and rosemary.

Prepare the grill. Place the focaccia over direct medium heat. Cook 14–16 minutes, turning once while cooking. Remove from the grill and cut into 2–3-inch squares. Serve immediately.

YIELD: **6–8 servings**

# Something Cool to Drink

# Sangria

2 oz brandy

4 oz dry red wine (Merlot or
    Cabernet)

1 oz simple syrup
    (1 cup water, 1 cup sugar,
    heated until sugar dissolves,
    then cooled)

1 oz orange juice

1 oz pineapple juice

Combine all and stir. Serve in a large wineglass garnished with slices of fresh fruit.

YIELD: 1 drink

# Gold Margaritas with Cointreau

1½ oz Jose Cuervo tequila

½ oz Cointreau

Splash of freshly squeezed lime
    juice

4 oz sweet and sour mix

Place all ingredients in a metal cocktail shaker with ice. Shake well. Serve in a salt-rimmed cocktail glass garnished with lime.

YIELD: 1 drink

OPPOSITE: Gold Margaritas with Cointreau

# The Purple Parrot Café Grapefruit-Basil Cocktail

9 large basil leaves, stems removed

1½ oz simple syrup (1 cup water, 1 cup sugar, heated until sugar dissolves, then cooled) (more if you are not using ruby red grapefruits)

1½ oz Tito's vodka

4 oz ruby red grapefruit juice, freshly squeezed

½ lime, cut into 4 wedges

Muddle basil leaves with simple syrup. Transfer to a metal cocktail shaker. Add Tito's vodka, grapefruit juice, and lime. Shake and strain over a cocktail glass filled with ice. Garnish with 1 basil leaf.

YIELD: 1 drink

# Mississippi Watermelon-Basil Martini

1 cup cubed watermelon

8 basil leaves

1¼ oz Tanqueray

½ oz simple syrup (1 cup water, 1 cup sugar, heated until sugar dissolves, then cooled)

2 lime wedges

Place all in a metal cocktail shaker with ice. Shake well. Strain into a martini glass.

YIELD: 1 drink

# Crescent City Grill Southern Sunset

3 oz fresh raspberries,
approximately 12
raspberries, may substitute
frozen

1 oz Jack Daniel's

½ oz Chambord

½ lime, cut into 4 wedges

4 oz cranberry juice

Muddle raspberries. Place in a metal cocktail shaker. Add ice, Jack Daniel's, Chambord, lime wedges, and cranberry juice. Shake well and strain into a cocktail glass filled with ice.

YIELD: 1 drink

# Pineapple Caipirinha

½ lime, cut into 4 wedges

1 oz simple syrup
(1 cup water, 1 cup sugar,
heated until sugar dissolves,
then cooled)

1½ oz Cachaça Coral

4 oz pineapple juice

1 pineapple wedge

Muddle lime wedges with simple syrup. Add Cachaça Coral and pineapple juice. Pour into a metal cocktail shaker, add ice, and shake lightly. Pour into a tall glass. Do not strain. Garnish with a pineapple wedge.

YIELD: 1 drink

# Seersucker

2 oz vodka

2 oz cranberry cocktail

1 oz simple syrup
    (1 cup water, 1 cup sugar,
    heated until sugar dissolves,
    then cooled)

2 tsp freshly squeezed lime
    juice

2 oz soda water

Lime slices

Place all ingredients in a metal cocktail shaker. Add ice. Cover and shake well. Serve in a Collins glass. Garnish with lime slices.

YIELD: 1 drink

# Raspberry Fizzle

3 oz fresh raspberries,
    approximately 12
    raspberries, may substitute
    frozen

1¼ oz Tanqueray No. 10 gin

¼ oz Pama Pomegranate
    Flavored Liqueur

½ lemon, cut into 4 wedges

1 egg white

1 oz simple syrup
    (1 cup water, 1 cup sugar,
    heated until sugar dissolves,
    then cooled)

Mint sprig

Muddle raspberries with gin. Place in a metal cocktail shaker. Add Pama, lemon wedges, egg white, and simple syrup. Shake well and strain into a chilled cocktail glass filled with ice. Garnish with a sprig of mint.

YIELD: 1 drink

OPPOSITE: Seersucker

# Flirtini

2 oz pineapple juice

2 oz vodka

1 oz sweet sparkling wine,
   such as Prosecco

Fill a metal cocktail shaker half full with ice. Add pineapple juice
and vodka. Cover and shake well. Strain into a martini glass and
float sparkling wine on top of drink.

YIELD: 1 drink

# Nail on the Head

½ oz Johnnie Walker Red
   Scotch

½ oz Drambuie

½ oz Kahlúa

2 oz half-and-half

3 coffee beans

Place all ingredients except coffee beans into a metal cocktail
shaker and shake well. Strain into a chilled martini glass. Garnish
with 3 coffee beans.

YIELD: 1 drink

# Purple Parrot Mint Julep

12 mint leaves

1 oz simple syrup
(1 cup water, 1 cup sugar,
heated until sugar dissolves,
then cooled)

1¼ oz Maker's Mark

2 oz soda water

3 dashes of Angostura bitters

Mint sprig

Muddle mint leaves with simple syrup. Place in a metal cocktail shaker filled half-full of ice. Add Maker's Mark, soda water, and bitters. Shake well. Pour into a cocktail glass. Do not strain. Garnish with a sprig of mint.

YIELD: 1 drink

# Julia's Julep

My friend Julia Reed serves these at her New Orleans Garden District home. She keeps the mint syrup in the refrigerator and adds it to chocolate when preparing a chocolate-mint dish.

1 bunch fresh mint, stems
removed

2 cups simple syrup (1 cup
water, 1 cup sugar, heated
until sugar dissolves)

2 oz bourbon

Crushed ice

Mint sprig

Steep the mint in the hot simple syrup for 2 hours. Strain. Fill a cocktail glass with crushed ice. Add 1 tablespoon of the mint syrup. Add bourbon. Garnish with a sprig of mint.

YIELD: 1 drink

# Not-Your-Grandmother's Mint Julep

6 mint leaves, plus 1 mint sprig

½ oz simple syrup
(1 cup water, 1 cup sugar, heated until sugar dissolves, then cooled)

2 oz bourbon

3 oz soda water

Crushed ice

Muddle mint together with the simple syrup. Pour into a cocktail glass. Add bourbon, soda water, and fill with ice. Garnish with a sprig of fresh mint.

YIELD: 1 drink

# Mint Condition

12 mint leaves, plus 1 sprig (or apple slice)

1½ oz Don Q rum

2 tsp honey

½ lime, cut into 4 wedges

3 oz apple juice

Muddle mint leaves with rum. Place in a metal cocktail shaker. Add honey and stir well with a long spoon. Add lime and apple juice and shake well. Strain into a chilled martini glass. Garnish with a slice of apple or sprig of mint.

YIELD: 1 drink

OPPOSITE: Not-Your-Grandmother's Mint Julep

*"The no-stick grilling marinades can also be used whenever you're grilling or sautéing: not just for the recipes in this book."*

# Seasonings, Rubs, Marinades, and Sauces

The no-stick grilling marinades have a great shelf life—at least 2 weeks. If you are thinning with water, only do so while the motor's running. Don't freak out about the strong flavors when tasted on their own. They are meant to accompany and season food items, not to be eaten as a stand-alone condiment. As with all recipes, freshly ground black pepper is a must.

Feel free to improvise with Worcestershire, soy sauce, flavored oils, and different mustard varieties to develop your own version of these flavoring marinades.

The no-stick grilling marinades can also be used whenever you're grilling or sautéing: not just for the recipes in this book.

Keep the no-stick grilling marinade in the refrigerator and use a firm pastry brush when applying.

*"As with all recipes, freshly ground black pepper is a must. Feel free to improvise . . . to develop your own version of these flavoring marinades."*

# No-stick Grilling Marinade for Beef

Brush this no-stick grilling marinade on burgers or steaks 30–45 minutes before grilling. A tarragon-flavored vinegar is a great substitute for the balsamic.

4 egg yolks

1 Tbl Dijon mustard

¼ cup balsamic vinegar

1 cup canola oil

1 cup light olive oil

Warm water as needed

2 Tbl Lawry's Seasoned Salt

2 Tbl freshly ground black pepper

2 Tbl lemon pepper seasoning

2 tsp garlic powder

1 tsp onion powder

Place the egg yolks, Dijon mustard, and vinegar in a food processor. Blend on medium speed for 1–2 minutes.

Slowly drizzle oils into the mixture, 1 tablespoon at a time. If the marinade becomes too thick, add 1–2 tablespoons of warm water. Once all of the oil has been incorporated, add seasoned salt, pepper, lemon pepper, garlic powder, and onion powder until incorporated. Store covered in the refrigerator until needed.

YIELD: 2½ cups

# No-stick Grilling Marinade for Poultry

Brush this no-stick grilling marinade on whole chicken, bone-in chicken pieces, or boneless-skinless breasts 30–45 minutes before grilling. You can also use it to pre-baste and season your Thanksgiving turkey. Dijon mustard is the perfect substitute for Creole or whole-grain mustard.

4 egg yolks

1 Tbl Creole or whole-grain mustard

¼ cup balsamic vinegar

1 cup canola oil

1 cup light olive oil

Warm water as needed

2 Tbl Lawry's Seasoned Salt

2 Tbl garlic powder

1 Tbl white pepper

2 Tbl lemon pepper seasoning

2 Tbl celery salt

Place the egg yolks, Creole mustard, and vinegar in a food processor. Blend on medium speed for 1–2 minutes.

Slowly drizzle oils into the mixture, 1 tablespoon at a time. If the marinade becomes too thick, add 1–2 tablespoons of warm water. Once all of the oil has been incorporated, add seasoned salt, garlic powder, white pepper, lemon pepper, and celery salt until incorporated.

Store covered in the refrigerator until needed.

YIELD: 2½ cups

# No-stick Grilling Marinade for Seafood

Fresh fish is one of the hardest proteins to grill. The no-stick marinade is perfect when grilling filets or whole fish. Brush the no-stick grilling marinade on fish, scallops, soft-shell crabs, or lobster 30–45 minutes before grilling.

4 egg yolks

1 Tbl Dijon mustard

¼ cup balsamic vinegar

1 cup canola oil

1 cup light olive oil

Warm water as needed

2 Tbl Lawry's Seasoned Salt

1 Tbl onion powder

1 Tbl paprika

½ tsp cayenne pepper

2 tsp garlic powder

1 tsp white pepper

1 tsp freshly ground black pepper

1 tsp dry mustard

1 tsp dry oregano

1 tsp dried thyme leaves

Place the egg yolks, Dijon mustard, and vinegar in a food processor. Blend on medium speed for 1–2 minutes.

Slowly drizzle oils into the mixture, 1 tablespoon at a time. If the marinade becomes too thick, add 1–2 tablespoons of warm water. Once all of the oil has been incorporated, add seasoned salt, onion powder, paprika, cayenne, garlic powder, white pepper, black pepper, dry mustard, oregano, and thyme until incorporated.

Store covered in the refrigerator until needed.

YIELD: **2½ cups**

# No-stick Grilling Marinade for Shrimp

Brush shrimp with no-stick grilling marinade 15–20 minutes before grilling. Or brush the shrimp and sauté in a skillet with butter, garlic, and fresh herbs for a great and easy scampi.

4 egg yolks

1 Tbl Dijon mustard

¼ cup balsamic vinegar

1 cup canola oil

1 cup light olive oil

Warm water as needed

2 Tbl Lawry's Seasoned Salt

¼ cup Old Bay seasoning

1 Tbl lemon pepper seasoning

Place the egg yolks, Dijon mustard, and vinegar in a food processor. Blend on medium speed for 1–2 minutes.

Slowly drizzle oils into the mixture, 1 tablespoon at a time. If the marinade becomes too thick, add 1–2 tablespoons of warm water. Once all of the oil has been incorporated, add seasoned salt, Old Bay seasoning, and lemon pepper, until incorporated.

Store covered in the refrigerator until needed.

YIELD: 2½ cups

# No-stick Grilling Marinade for Vegetables

Brush the no-stick grilling marinade on vegetables 30–45 minutes before grilling. Use a lemon-and-dill-flavored oil or an herb-flavored oil.

4 egg yolks

1 Tbl yellow mustard

¼ cup balsamic vinegar

1 cup canola oil

1 cup light olive oil

Warm water as needed

2 Tbl Lawry's Seasoned Salt

2 Tbl garlic powder

2 Tbl onion powder

1 Tbl lemon pepper seasoning

1 Tbl celery salt

½ tsp freshly ground black pepper

Place the egg yolks, mustard, and vinegar in a food processor. Blend on medium speed for 1–2 minutes.

Slowly drizzle oils into the mixture, 1 tablespoon at a time. If the marinade becomes too thick, add 1–2 tablespoons of warm water. Once all of the oil has been incorporated, add seasoned salt, garlic powder, onion powder, lemon pepper, celery salt, and black pepper until incorporated.

Store covered in the refrigerator until needed.

YIELD: 2½ cups

# Steak Seasoning

Make your own and give as gifts. Use this on burgers and all types of beef.

½ cup Lawry's Seasoned Salt

¾ cup freshly ground black
    pepper

¼ cup lemon pepper seasoning

2 Tbl garlic salt

2 Tbl granulated garlic

1 Tbl onion powder

Combine all the ingredients and mix well. Store in an airtight container.

YIELD: 1⅓ cups

# BBQ Seasoning

Works on all cuts of pork, beef, and chicken.

⅓ cup Lawry's Seasoned Salt

⅓ cup paprika

2 Tbl onion powder

2 Tbl cayenne pepper

1 Tbl white pepper

5 tsp garlic powder

1 Tbl freshly ground black
    pepper

1 Tbl dry mustard

1 tsp oregano

1 tsp thyme

Mix all the ingredients thoroughly.

YIELD: 1 cup

# Creole Seasoning

I use this as I would salt. My friend, and the talented photographer who shot all of the food in this book, Joey DeLeo, spent three weeks in South Mississippi while shooting the photographs. He ate in our restaurants dozens of times. On a return visit from New York, he was craving the food: "It has a certain flavor that I just love." He was talking about the Creole Seasoning.

½ cup Lawry's Seasoned Salt

2 Tbl onion powder

2 Tbl paprika

1 Tbl cayenne

1 Tbl white pepper

1 Tbl plus 1 tsp garlic powder

1 Tbl freshly ground black
    pepper

1 tsp dry mustard

1 tsp dry oregano

1 tsp dry thyme

Combine all ingredients.

YIELD: 1 cup

# Poultry Seasoning

Use when grilling, sautéing, or roasting chicken or turkey. Good for fried chicken, and works well on oven-baked French fries, too.

¼ cup Lawry's Seasoned Salt

¼ cup garlic powder

¼ cup white pepper

¼ cup lemon pepper seasoning

¼ cup celery salt

Combine and mix well. Store in an airtight container.

YIELD: 1¼ cups

*"··· works well on oven-baked French fries, too."*

# Comeback Sauce

The ultimate Mississippi condiment. It's a dip, it's a spread, it's a salad dressing, and it's great when dipped with crackers, as they do in the old-line Greek restaurants in Jackson. Add more garlic if you dare.

1 cup mayonnaise
½ cup ketchup
½ cup chili sauce
½ cup cottonseed oil
½ cup grated yellow onions
3 Tbl lemon juice
2 Tbl minced garlic
1 Tbl paprika
1 Tbl water
1 Tbl Worcestershire sauce
1 tsp freshly ground black
    pepper
½ tsp dry mustard
1 tsp salt

Combine all the ingredients in a food processor and mix well.

YIELD: 3½ cups

*"The ultimate Mississippi condiment.*
*It's a dip, it's a spread, it's a salad dressing . . ."*

# Roasted Garlic Bordelaise

If you don't want to make Veal Stock, or if you have trouble finding veal bones, find a good veal demi-glace at your local gourmet food store.

2 Tbl unsalted butter

½ cup small dice yellow onions

⅓ cup small dice carrots

¼ cup small dice celery

2 tsp minced fresh garlic

½ tsp salt

2 Tbl tomato paste

½ tsp freshly ground black pepper

1 cup dry red wine

1 bay leaf

1 quart Veal Stock or rich beef stock (page 158)

⅓ cup Roasted Garlic Puree (page 42)

1 tsp chopped fresh thyme leaves

Heat butter in a 2-quart sauce pot over medium heat. Add onions, carrots, celery, garlic, and salt, and cook until vegetables soften, 5–6 minutes. Add tomato paste and black pepper, stir constantly, and cook for 5–6 minutes. Using a wire whisk, stir in red wine and bay leaf.

Simmer until wine has reduced by half. Add Veal Stock and bring to a boil. Reduce the heat to low medium and simmer, slowly, until reduced by half, 1–1½ hours.

Adjust the seasoning and keep warm until ready to serve. Stir in the Roasted Garlic Puree and fresh thyme and remove the bay leaf just before serving.

YIELD: 3 cups

# Lemon-Garlic Beurre Blanc

A very versatile sauce, which can be used with chicken, beef, seafood, and pasta. Change the flavor profile by adding freshly chopped herbs once all of the butter has been incorporated.

⅔ cup white wine

⅓ cup white vinegar

⅓ cup fresh lemon juice

½ cup finely chopped shallots

2 Tbl minced garlic

¼ cup whipping cream

1½ cups unsalted butter, cut into small cubes, then chilled

1 tsp salt

In a small saucepan over medium heat, reduce wine, vinegar, lemon juice, shallots, and garlic until almost all liquid has evaporated. Add cream and reduce by half. Reduce heat.

Incorporate the butter a few pieces at a time. Stir constantly using a wire whisk until butter is completely melted. When butter is incorporated, remove from heat, strain, and keep in a warm (not hot) area until needed. Add salt to taste.

YIELD: 1½ cups

# Lemon Meunière Sauce

Great with fish, beef, or veal.

⅔ cup white wine

2 Tbl white vinegar

⅓ cup reduced Veal Stock (page 158)

2 Tbl lemon juice

½ cup finely chopped shallots

¼ cup whipping cream

1½ cups unsalted butter, cut into small cubes, then chilled

1 tsp salt

In a small saucepan over medium heat, reduce wine, vinegar, Veal Stock, lemon juice, and shallots. When almost all liquid has evaporated, add cream. Allow cream to reduce by half. Reduce heat slightly and incorporate the butter a few pieces at a time. Stir constantly using a wire whisk until butter is completely melted. When all butter is incorporated, remove from heat. Strain and keep in a warm (not hot) area until needed.

YIELD: 2 cups

# Clarified Butter

Good to have on hand to substitute for cooking oil when sautéing. It's a great way to add butter flavor to a dish without having to deal with the low smoke point of unclarified butter.

3 lbs butter

Place butter in a heavy 2-quart saucepan over medium heat. Adjust heat as butter melts to bubbling. As butter cooks, skim the white foam with a spoon and discard. Over time, the bubbles will get smaller and the butter will become clear. Once clear, remove from the heat.

Allow to cool 1 hour, and pour through a fine-mesh strainer or cheesecloth. Discard any water or solids left at the bottom.

YIELD: 4 cups

# BBQ Sauce

This sauce has a good shelf life. Double the recipe and freeze the other half, so you'll always have some on hand.

2 Tbl bacon fat

2 Tbl dehydrated onions

2 tsp minced fresh garlic

¼ cup brown sugar

¼ cup sugar

¼ cup molasses

2 cups chicken stock

1 quart ketchup

1½ Tbl freshly ground black
  pepper

¼ tsp cayenne pepper

2 Tbl dry mustard

2 Tbl lemon juice

¼ cup Worcestershire sauce

½ cup balsamic vinegar

½ cup cider vinegar

Preheat oven to 300 degrees.

In a 3-quart Dutch oven, heat the bacon fat over low heat. Add the dehydrated onions and garlic and cook for 3–4 minutes. Stir in the remaining ingredients and place the sauce in the oven. Bake for 2 hours, stirring every 15 minutes.

Use to baste ribs during the last hour of cooking, or serve on the side.

YIELD: 8–10 servings

# Ginger Soy Sauce

A longtime staple in the Purple Parrot kitchens; it takes an extra step, but freshly squeezed orange juice makes a huge difference in the outcome of the recipe.

2 cups orange juice

½ cup rice wine vinegar

½ cup white wine

1 Tbl minced garlic

1 Tbl minced shallots

1 orange, cut into slices

2 Tbl chopped fresh ginger
(it is not necessary to peel)

1 jalapeño, seeds removed and
roughly chopped

¼ cup whipping cream

1½ cups unsalted butter,
cut into small cubes,
then chilled

2 Tbl soy sauce

In a medium saucepan, place orange juice, vinegar, wine, garlic, shallots, orange, ginger, and jalapeño over medium heat, and reduce to a thick syrup. Be careful; mixture burns easily.

Lower heat and add cream. Bring mixture back to a simmer. Start adding butter, stirring constantly. Add more butter as it dissolves, until all butter is incorporated. Strain through a fine-mesh strainer and finish with soy sauce.

YIELD: 2 cups

# Roasted Tomato Tartar Sauce

This recipe came from my love of combining cocktail sauce and tartar sauce when eating fried crab claws.

1 large ripe tomato, halved

1 Tbl olive oil

¼ tsp kosher salt

1¼ cups mayonnaise

2 Tbl sweet pickle relish

1 Tbl yellow mustard

2 Tbl chopped capers

2 Tbl chopped green olives

1½ tsp freshly ground black
    pepper

1 tsp minced fresh garlic

½ tsp garlic salt

1½ tsp parsley

1 Tbl freshly squeezed lemon
    juice

Preheat oven to 350 degrees.

Rub the tomato halves with olive oil and sprinkle with the salt. Place tomato halves on a small baking dish. Bake 15 minutes, turn over, and bake for 10 minutes more. (The tomato should start to turn slightly brown.) Remove and cool completely.

Once the tomato has cooled, roughly chop it.

Combine tomato with remaining ingredients, mix well, and refrigerate 4 to 6 hours before serving.

YIELD: 2½ cups

# Creole Beurre Rouge

If you don't use freshly made chicken stock, make sure to substitute a low-sodium chicken broth or base. Works with shrimp, fish, and chicken, too.

1 Tbl olive oil

2 Tbl small dice green peppers

¼ cup small dice yellow onions

1 Tbl minced garlic

¼ cup small dice celery

2 tsp Creole Seasoning (page 212)

1½ cups medium dice tomatoes

1 cup white wine

1 cup chicken stock

2 Tbl white vinegar

1 bay leaf

1 tsp dried oregano

1 cup unsalted butter, cubed and kept cold until needed

1 tsp freshly ground black pepper

1 Tbl chopped fresh thyme

In a medium sauce pot, heat olive oil over medium high heat. Sauté peppers, onions, garlic, celery, and Creole Seasoning for 5 minutes. Add tomatoes and cook 5 minutes longer. Add wine and reduce by half. Add chicken stock, vinegar, bay leaf, and oregano, and simmer 15–20 minutes, until the sauce turns into a thick paste.

Lower the heat, and using a wire whisk, begin incorporating the butter cubes, 2–3 at a time. Stir constantly to prevent the sauce from separating. Once all butter is added, stir in the black pepper and thyme, and remove from the heat. Remove and discard the bay leaf.

Store in a warm place (120 degrees) until needed.

YIELD: 6–8 servings

# Cucumber-Dill Dressing

Light and refreshing. Can be used as a dip or spread on petite bread for tomato sandwiches. Best if made one day in advance.

1 cup plain yogurt (do not use low-fat or nonfat)

1 cucumber (about 16 oz), peeled, halved lengthwise, and seeded

½ cup mayonnaise

½ tsp kosher salt

⅛ tsp freshly ground black pepper

1 tsp lemon juice

1 tsp white wine vinegar

3 Tbl finely chopped fresh dill

2 tsp minced fresh garlic

Place a strainer over a large bowl. Line strainer with 3 layers of cheesecloth. Spoon yogurt into cheesecloth-lined strainer; let stand at room temperature to drain 3 hours (liquid will drain out and yogurt will thicken).

Transfer yogurt to a medium bowl; discard liquid. Meanwhile, coarsely grate cucumber. Place in another strainer; let stand at room temperature until most of liquid drains out, about 3 hours. Discard liquid. Squeeze excess moisture from cucumber.

Combine all the ingredients. Cover and refrigerate.

YIELD: 1½ cups

# Seafood Rémoulade

The ultimate condiment for grilled, broiled, sautéed, and fried seafood. Can be used when making fried shrimp or oyster po-boys or as a dressing for a chilled shrimp salad. Best if made at least 1 day in advance. Sauce holds up to 1 week in the refrigerator.

⅓ cup chopped onions

1 celery stalk

1 cup ketchup

3 Tbl freshly squeezed lemon juice

1 tsp Creole mustard

¼ cup prepared horseradish

1 cup mayonnaise

2 tsp Creole Seasoning (page 212)

1 tsp Lawry's Seasoned Salt

1 tsp minced garlic

Blend onions and celery in the food processor until small but not completely puréed. Place onions and celery in a mixing bowl.

Add remaining ingredients and mix well.

YIELD: 2 cups

*"The ultimate condiment for grilled, broiled, sautéed, and fried seafood."*

# Dijon-Horseradish Sauce

Great for all types of beef sandwiches and entrées.

2 Tbl yellow mustard

¼ cup prepared horseradish

¾ cup Dijon mustard

¼ cup honey

2 Tbl bourbon

1 Tbl ketchup

1 Tbl red wine vinegar

1 Tbl chopped parsley

1 tsp chopped fresh thyme

1 tsp freshly ground black
    pepper

Mix together all the ingredients. For the best flavor, prepare and refrigerate the mustard a day in advance. Allow the mustard to get to room temperature before serving.

YIELD: 1½ cups

# Deep South Steak Sauce

Purists scoff at anyone who would use a steak sauce, and I agree that the usual suspects that come in a bottle and are used by restaurant customers to try to add more flavor to well-done steaks are never acceptable. This is an excellent and legitimate exception.

½ cup butter (1 stick)

¼ cup Worcestershire sauce

1 Tbl A.1. steak sauce

1 tsp Liquid Smoke

1 tsp hot sauce

2 tsp Steak Seasoning
    (page 211)

Melt butter over medium low heat and add remaining ingredients. Stir well and serve with grilled steaks.

YIELD: 1 cup

# Smoky Fajita Sauce

It doesn't look pretty, but it tastes great with fajitas. This recipe came from my fajita-eating habit of blending BBQ sauce and sour cream as the base when building a fajita. This sauce is simple and great just like it is. For variations, you can add ¼ cup of salsa to it. Or try adding fresh chopped cilantro and green onions, or 1 teaspoon of Liquid Smoke.

¾ cup sour cream
¾ cup BBQ Sauce (page 220)

Mix together and chill before serving.

YIELD: 1½ cups

*"Peaches taste like summer. Georgia and South Carolina fight over which state is the best peach grower."*

# Something Sweet

# Caramelized Pineapple with Pineapple Sherbet

Pineapple sherbet was my favorite as a kid. It's great in summer. When choosing pineapple, the sweeter the better. Golden pineapples work best. If you don't have an ice cream maker, place the ingredients in a Ziploc bag in the freezer. Turn and squish every 30 minutes until solid.

1 whole ripe pineapple
½ cup unsalted butter
⅔ cup sugar

Place the pineapple on its side and cut off about ½ inch from the top and the bottom. Stand the pineapple upright and cut lengthwise to remove the tough outer skin. After the skin has been removed, shave off any remaining hard bits of peel. Cut the pineapple in quarters, lengthwise, through the core. Lay each quarter flat and, slicing at an angle, remove the hard center core. Cut each quarter in half lengthwise again, rendering 8 long, slender pieces of pineapple.

Prepare grill for medium heat direct cooking.

Melt butter in a medium-sized sauté pan. Stir in the sugar and cook just until the sugar begins to dissolve. Using about one quarter of this mixture, lightly brush the surfaces of the pineapple. Grill for 8–10 minutes, turning once.

Serve with Pineapple Sherbet (recipe follows).

YIELD: 8–12 slices

(continued)

# Pineapple Sherbet

1 can sweetened condensed
   milk

1 whole pineapple, peeled,
   core removed, and cut into
   chunks

½ cup cold milk

2 tsp fresh lemon juice

Place the sweetened condensed milk and the pineapple chunks in a blender and puree until very smooth. Pass the mixture through a fine-mesh strainer, pressing firmly. Discard the remaining pulp. Stir the milk and lemon juice into the pineapple puree, and chill for 30 minutes.

Freeze the sherbet following the manufacturer's directions of your ice cream maker. Place it in an airtight container and cover. Freeze at least 1 hour before serving.

YIELD: 1 quart

# Grilled Peach Shortcake with Peach Ice Cream

Peaches taste like summer. Georgia and South Carolina fight over which state is the best peach grower. Personally, I like the ones that are grown in Chilton County, Alabama. They always seem to arrive early. The shortcake recipe works well for strawberry shortcake or any other fruit-topped dessert (or eaten on its own as a sweet biscuit).

2 cups all-purpose flour

2 Tbl plus ¾ cup sugar, plus extra for sprinkling

1 Tbl baking powder

⅛ tsp salt

¾ cup cold unsalted butter (1½ sticks), diced

3 large eggs, lightly beaten

¼ cup heavy cream, chilled

¼ cup sour cream

1½ tsp vanilla extract

Egg wash (1 egg beaten with 2 Tbl water or milk )

6 large ripe peaches, peeled and halved

¼ cup melted butter

2 tsp lemon juice

Peach Ice Cream (recipe follows)

Preheat oven to 375 degrees.

Sift the flour, 2 tablespoons of the sugar, the baking powder, and salt into the bowl of an electric mixer fitted with the paddle attachment. Blend in butter at the lowest speed and mix until the butter is the size of peas. Combine eggs, heavy cream, sour cream, and 1 teaspoon of the vanilla, and quickly add to the flour and butter mixture. Mix until just blended. The dough will be sticky.

Dump the dough out onto a well-floured surface. Flour your hands and pat the dough out to ¾ inch thick. You should see lumps of butter in the dough.

Cut biscuits with a 3–4-inch cutter and place on a baking sheet lined with parchment.

Brush the tops with the egg wash. Sprinkle with sugar and bake 18–20 minutes, until the outsides are crisp and the insides are fully baked. Let cool on a wire rack.

Prepare the grill. Brush the peaches with melted butter. Cook peaches, flat side down, over direct medium heat, for 10 minutes. Rotate the peaches a quarter turn after 3 minutes, then

(continued)

turn them over once after 6 minutes of cooking. Remove the peaches from the grill and toss them in a bowl with the ¾ cup of the sugar, the lemon juice, and the remaining vanilla. Cover and keep warm until needed.

Split shortcakes in half and top each with a scoop of Peach Ice Cream. Place a warm peach half on the ice cream and top with the remaining shortcake halves. Drizzle the syrup from the bowl with the peaches over the shortcakes, and serve immediately.

YIELD: 6–8 servings

## Peach Ice Cream

3 cups fresh, peeled peach wedges, 8–10 wedges from each peach (can use frozen)

¾ cup sugar

1 Tbl lemon juice

¼ cup peach Schnapps

1½ cups whipping cream

1 cup milk

2 tsp vanilla extract

4 egg yolks

The perfect finish for an outdoor grilling party or picnic. When choosing peaches for this recipe, err on the side of the overripe ones.

In a bowl, combine peaches, ¼ cup of the sugar, lemon juice, and peach Schnapps. Allow the peaches to sit in mixture 10 minutes. Remove the peach wedges and reserve the sugar mixture.

Prepare the grill. Cook peaches 10 minutes over direct medium heat, turning once. Cut peaches into small pieces and return to the sugar mixture. Cover and refrigerate overnight.

Remove peach mixture from refrigerator, drain, and reserve the juice. Return peaches to refrigerator.

Place the liquid from the peaches, whipping cream, milk, and vanilla in a small sauce pot. Heat until the liquid comes to a simmer.

In a bowl, whisk egg yolks and remaining sugar. While whisking, slowly add one third of the boiled cream mixture. Stir well. Add egg mixture to cream mixture. Return to low medium heat

and continue stirring for 5–7 minutes. Just as it begins to simmer, remove from heat and place into a bowl over ice. Stir the cooling mixture often until completely chilled.

Transfer the mixture to an ice cream maker and freeze according to manufacturer's instructions. After the ice cream begins to stiffen, add the peaches and continue to freeze until done. Remove the ice cream from the ice cream maker and store in an airtight container in the freezer until ready to serve.

YIELD: 1 quart

# Grilled Bananas Foster

When preparing this recipe, err on the side of unripened bananas so that they are firm and easier to grill.

6 ripe bananas

⅓ cup plus 2 Tbl unsalted butter

1 cup plus 2 Tbl brown sugar

¾ tsp cinnamon

Pinch of nutmeg

1 cup dark rum

vanilla ice cream

Peel the bananas and cut in half lengthwise. Melt 2 tablespoons of the butter.

Brush the bananas with the melted butter and sprinkle them with 2 tablespoons of the brown sugar.

Prepare the grill. Cook bananas over direct high heat 4–6 minutes, turning once. Remove bananas from the grill and hold.

Melt the remaining butter in a large skillet over medium heat. Add the remaining brown sugar, the cinnamon, and nutmeg, and cook until the sugar dissolves, stirring constantly. Add rum and gently move the pan around to warm the rum, causing it to flame. Continue cooking until the flame dies out. Add the grilled bananas to the hot rum mixture and cook 3–4 minutes more.

To serve, place a large scoop of vanilla ice cream onto each of 6 serving dishes. Place 2 banana halves over the ice cream and drizzle with some of the sauce.

YIELD: 6 servings

Robert with food photographer Joey DeLeo

# Index

not-your-grandmother's mint
  julep, 200
pineapple caipirinha, 195
The Purple Parrot Café grapefruit-
  basil cocktail, 194
Purple Parrot mint julep, 199
raspberry fizzle, 197
sangria, 193
seersucker, 197

# E

eggplant, grilled, 85
equipment and tools, 5, 7

# F

fajita(s):
  marinated beef and chicken, with
    smoky fajita sauce, 179–80
  sauce, smoky, 229
fish, 5
  bayou redfish, 131
  cold-smoked tuna steaks with
    smoked vegetables, 104–5
  ginger soy salmon, 106
  grilled, tacos with three sauces,
    11–13
  grilled cioppino, 109–10
  grilled grouper Madeira, 126
  grilled redfish sandwiches with
    seafood rémoulade sauce, 60
  grouper with black bean, corn,
    and tomato salsa, 97–98
  marinated cedar-plank salmon, 99

no-stick grilling marinade
  for, 208
pompano in a foil bag, 100
redfish on the half shell with
  lemon garlic beurre blanc, 102
redfish Orleans, 128–29
smoked tuna pasta salad, 73–74
snapper Pontchartrain, 125
yellowfin tuna kabobs, 37
see also shellfish
flirtini, 198
focaccia, grilled, 190

# G

garlic:
  cheese grits, grilled shrimp
    over, 118
  croutons, 44
  -lemon beurre blanc, 217
  lemon beurre blanc, redfish on
    the half shell with, 102
  -lemon pepper oysters, grilled
    roasted, 41–42
  roasted, and jalapeño crème
    fraîche, 15
  roasted, bordelaise, 216
  roasted, bordelaise, cowboy
    ribeyes with tobacco onions
    and, 160
  roasted, mayonnaise, 57
  roasted, mint compound butter,
    grilled lamb chops with, 183–84
  roasted, puree, 42
  -Romano oysters, grilled, 40

meats (*continued*)

    smoked eye of round sandwich, 53

    steak seasoning for, 211

    tenderloin with sizzling butter, 173

    whole grilled tenderloin with chive-tarragon mayonnaise, 155–56

    whole smoked prime rib, 162

mint:

    condition, 200

    Julia's julep, 199

    julep, not-your-grandmother's, 200

    julep, Purple Parrot, 199

    raspberry sauce, grilled leg of lamb with, 181–82

    -roasted garlic compound butter, grilled lamb chops with, 183–84

molasses-glazed ham steaks, 147

mushroom(s):

    Basin Street chicken, 137

    Big Easy chicken sandwiches, 62

    grilled grouper Madeira, 126

    marinated and grilled, 90

    portobello, shrimp-stuffed, 83

    redfish Orleans, 128–29

    risotto, skewered scallops over, 120–23

    and shrimp quesadillas, 17

    -Swiss burgers with Dijon-horseradish sauce, 49

mustard, Dijon:

    cognac sauce, cracked-pepper burgers with, 52

    cognac sauce, cracked pepper filet with, 157–58

    honey-spiked, 56

    -horseradish sauce, 228

    -horseradish sauce, mushroom-Swiss burgers with, 49

# N

nail on the head, 198

# O

olives:

    basil tapenade, 24

    pasta salad, 45

onions:

    Basin Street chicken, 137

    Big Easy chicken sandwiches, 62

    caramelized, 88

    cold-smoked tuna steaks with smoked vegetables, 104–5

    grilled redfish sandwiches with seafood rémoulade sauce, 60

    grilled Vidalia, 78

    tobacco, 91

    tobacco, cowboy ribeyes with a roasted garlic bordelaise and, 160

oranges:

    fresh fruit pico de gallo, 15

    whole roasted citrus chicken, 136